*easy*italian

easy italian

simple recipes for every occasion

maxine clark

RYLAND
PETERS
& SMALL

LONDON NEW YORK

Designer Sarah Fraser

Commissioning Editor Elsa Petersen-Schepelern

Editor Sharon Cochrane

Picture Research Emily Westlake

Production Sheila Smith

Art Director Gabriella Le Grazie

Publishing Director Alison Starling

Index Hilary Bird

First published in Great Britain in 2005
by Ryland Peters & Small
20–21 Jockey's Fields
London WC1R 4BW
www.rylandpeters.com

10 9 8 7 6 5 4 3 2 1

ISBN 1 84172 949 3

A CIP catalogue record for this book is available from
the British Library.

Printed in China

Notes

All spoon measurements are level unless otherwise
specified.

Ingredients for these recipes are available from larger
supermarkets, specialist greengrocers and delicatessens.

All eggs are medium unless otherwise specified.
Uncooked or partly cooked eggs should not be
served to the very young, the very old, those with
compromised immune systems or to pregnant women.

Ovens should be preheated to the specified temperature.
If using a fan-assisted oven, cooking times should be
reduced according to the manufacturer's instructions.

All the recipes in this book are by Maxine Clark with the
exception of those listed on page 240, which are by
Silvana Franco.

contents

simple, but delicious   *6*

antipasti and snacks   *8*

soup   *40*

risotto   *52*

pasta and polenta   *72*

pizzas, tarts and bread   *100*

salads, vegetables and pulses   *122*

fish   *164*

meat and poultry   *180*

sweet things   *196*

basics   *224*

index   *236*

credits   *240*

simple, but delicious

I think the reason I fell in love with Italy and Italian food is the relaxed, informal attitude shown towards cooking and entertaining. Any occasion seems to merit a meal that is lovingly prepared, to be shared by all whether friends or family.

On a recent trip to Sicily, I met some people at a wine tasting who insisted that I joined them for a meal the next day. This wasn't anything grand, but two families got together and, like a well-oiled machine, produced a wonderful meal of home-grown and pickled olives, fresh warm ricotta, salame, *pasta con le sarde* (pasta with wild fennel and fresh sardines), crusty semolina bread with their own new olive oil and their own wine. I took a *cassata* (a chilled sponge cake filled with sweetened ricotta, chocolate and candied fruit) from their local cake shop for pudding. The meal couldn't have been simpler. These were busy people who, with great ease, produced a banquet from a handful of fresh ingredients.

This is the key to cooking good Italian food – keep it simple and use the best and freshest ingredients. Italian cooking is not complicated, it is the combinations of flavours and textures that make it so approachable. There are no special, over-complicated cooking techniques – some dishes are cooked very quickly, retaining the bright fresh flavour of the ingredients, while some are cooked very slowly, releasing hidden depths and tenderizing the toughest cuts of meat to melting softness.

The recipes in this book are easily prepared and so suitable for our hectic lifestyles, resulting in food that is both warm and satisfying to eat and big on flavour. Take it easy with *Easy Italian*!

antipasti and snacks

During the season, asparagus in all its varieties – from purple-tipped, to green, or white (the beloved one) – is often served with egg in some form, especially in the north of Italy. To our taste, asparagus is overcooked in Italy, but this is how they serve it and I must say, the slightly longer cooking does bring out the flavour. Truffle oil is an optional luxury – you could add some chopped tarragon to the cream instead – but it is wonderful.

asparagus *with egg and truffle butter*

Hard-boil the eggs for about 10 minutes, depending on size. Let cool in cold water, then peel. Cut the eggs in half and remove the yolks. Finely chop the whites and reserve. Mash the yolks with the butter until well blended. Add a drop or two of truffle oil, if using, and season with salt. Cover and keep at room temperature.

Trim the asparagus. Steam it for about 12 minutes until tender. Arrange on 4 warm plates, sprinkle with the chopped egg white, salt and pepper, then serve with the golden butter. (The butter can either be spooned on top of the asparagus or served in little dishes to spread over each mouthful.)

4 free-range eggs

100 g unsalted butter, softened

a little truffle oil (optional)

500 g fresh asparagus

sea salt and freshly ground black pepper

serves 4

This speciality of Genoa in Liguria uses anchovies as a way of adding savoury saltiness, as fish sauce does in South-east Asian cooking. It doesn't taste overly fishy, but gives the earthy spinach a depth it would not have otherwise. The combination of salt (anchovies) and sweet (dried fruit), coupled with mild, creamy pine nuts in savoury dishes is common all over Italy.

spinach *with anchovies and pine nuts*

1 kg fresh spinach

100 ml good olive oil

4 anchovy fillets in oil, drained and chopped

3 tablespoons chopped fresh flat leaf parsley

3 tablespoons dried currants or small raisins, soaked in warm water for 15 minutes

4 tablespoons pine nuts

freshly grated nutmeg

sea salt and freshly ground black pepper

serves 4

Tear the stems off the spinach and discard them. Wash the leaves very well in plenty of cold water to remove any grit and sand. Shake dry in a colander or salad spinner, but leave some water clinging to the leaves.

Put the leaves in a saucepan, cover and cook for a few minutes until they wilt. Drain well in a colander but do not squeeze dry – you need large pieces of spinach.

Warm the oil in a large frying pan, add the chopped anchovies and parsley and stir for 2–3 minutes over medium heat until the anchovies dissolve. Add the spinach, drained currants and pine nuts. Add a good grating of nutmeg, taste, season with salt and pepper to taste and stir-fry for about 5 minutes until heated through, glossy and well mixed. Serve immediately.

courgette and mint fritters

600 g courgettes

finely grated zest of
1 unwaxed lemon

2 tablespoons chopped
fresh mint leaves

oil, for frying

sea salt and freshly
ground black pepper

lemon wedges, to serve

batter

2 eggs, separated

2 tablespoons olive oil

200 ml beer, such as lager

140 g plain flour

sea salt and freshly
ground black pepper

*an electric deep-fryer
(optional)*

serves 4

My favourite way with courgettes! It changes
their watery blandness into sweet and crunchy
mouthfuls with just a hint of mint. The batter
is light and, if fried at the correct temperature,
it doesn't absorb any oil at all.

To make the batter, put the egg yolks in a bowl, beat well,
then slowly beat in the oil, followed by the beer, then the
flour. Season with salt and pepper to taste. Cover and let
rest for 1 hour.

Meanwhile, grate the courgettes coarsely, sprinkle with
salt and toss well. Put them in a sieve and let drain for
10 minutes. Rinse them well, then pat dry with kitchen
paper. Put them in a bowl, add the lemon zest, mint, salt
and pepper and stir well.

Just before cooking, put the egg whites, salt and pepper in
a bowl and whisk until firm. Gently fold into the batter. Heat
the oil to 190°C (375°F) in a deep-fryer or saucepan with a
frying basket. Mix the grated courgettes with enough batter
to bind them.

Working in batches, slide about 6 small spoonfuls at a time
into the hot oil and fry for 2–3 minutes until golden and
crisp. Drain the fritters on kitchen paper, sprinkle with salt
and serve hot with lemon wedges.

Caponata is rather like ratatouille, but much more exotic. There are dozens of variations of this delectable dish from Sicily. It improves with age, so make a big batch and keep it in the refrigerator or preserve in large jars. It's served as an antipasto, but is delicious with grilled fish or steak. As always in Sicily and in hot weather, serve at room temperature – it tastes much better.

sweet and sour sicilian aubergine stew

4 medium aubergines, cut into bite-sized cubes

4 tablespoons olive oil

1 onion, chopped

2 celery stalks, sliced

12 very ripe large tomatoes, coarsely chopped, or 600 g canned chopped tomatoes

1–2 tablespoons salted capers, rinsed well

100 g best green olives, pitted

2 tablespoons red wine vinegar

2 teaspoons sugar

vegetable oil, for frying

sea salt

to serve

200 g fresh ricotta cheese

toasted chopped almonds

chopped fresh flat leaf parsley

an electric deep-fryer (optional)

serves 6

Put the aubergines in a colander, sprinkle with salt and let drain for 30 minutes.

Meanwhile, heat the olive oil in a saucepan and add the onion and celery. Cook for 5 minutes until softened but not browned, add the tomatoes, then cook for 15 minutes until pulpy. Add the capers, olives, vinegar and sugar to the sauce and cook for a further 15 minutes.

Rinse the aubergine cubes and pat them dry with kitchen paper.

Heat the vegetable oil in a deep-fryer to 190°C (375°F), add the aubergine cubes in batches and fry until deep golden brown. This may take some time, but cook them thoroughly, because undercooked aubergine is unpleasant. Alternatively, toss the cubes in olive oil, spread them in a roasting tin and roast at 200°C (400°F) Gas 6 for 20 minutes or until well browned and tender. Drain well.

Stir the aubergines into the sauce. Taste and adjust the seasoning (this means adding more sugar or vinegar to taste to balance the flavours). Set aside for at least 30 minutes or preferably overnight to develop the flavours before serving. Serve warm or at room temperature (never refrigerator-cold) in a shallow bowl and top with the ricotta, almonds and chopped parsley.

Very simple, this dish relies on pan-grilling the aubergines perfectly. Make sure you baste them with plenty of oil, and don't let the pan get too hot or the aubergines will burn before they brown – they should gently sizzle. Add a little crushed or chopped garlic to the dressing if you like, but the mint and lemon flavours are quite delicate.

pan-grilled aubergines *with lemon, mint and balsamic vinegar*

To make the dressing, put the oil, lemon juice and zest and balsamic vinegar in a bowl and whisk well. Add the sugar, salt and pepper to taste – it should be fairly sweet. Stir in half the mint, then set aside.

Heat a ridged stove-top grill pan until hot or light a barbecue and wait for the coals to turn white. Cut each aubergine into 8 thin slices, brush lightly with olive oil, add to the pan or barbecue and cook for 2–3 minutes on each side until golden brown and lightly charred. Arrange the slices on a large platter and spoon the dressing over the top. Cover and set aside to let the aubergines absorb the flavours of the dressing. Sprinkle with the remaining chopped mint and serve.

2 medium aubergines, about 500 g

olive oil, for basting

dressing

100 ml extra virgin olive oil

finely grated zest and juice of 1 unwaxed lemon

2 tablespoons balsamic vinegar

1–2 teaspoons sugar

4 tablespoons very coarsely chopped fresh mint leaves

sea salt and freshly ground black pepper

a stove-top grill pan or barbecue

serves 4

marinated fresh anchovies

There's nothing quite like these light, fresh, silvery morsels eaten fillet by fillet with a glass of chilled *vino bianco*, overlooking a peacock sea, with a warm salty breeze on your face. If you've never tried a fresh anchovy before and you see them in a market, buy them. They are mild and fresh, and the combination of lemon, parsley and olive oil is lifted by the zing of spring onion.

16 fresh anchovies, small sardines or sprats

freshly squeezed juice of 2 lemons

2 fat spring onions, thinly sliced

2 tablespoons chopped fresh flat leaf parsley

extra virgin olive oil

sea salt and freshly ground black pepper

serves 4

To clean the anchovies, cut off the heads and slit open the bellies. Remove the insides (there isn't very much there at all) under running water. Slide your thumb along the backbone to release the flesh along its length. Take hold of the backbone at the head end and lift it out. The fish should now open up like a book. At this stage you can decide whether to cut it into 2 long fillets or leave it whole – size will dictate. Pat them dry with kitchen paper.

Put the lemon juice in a shallow non-reactive dish and add the anchovies in an even layer, skin side up. Cover and let marinate in the refrigerator for 24 hours.

The next day, lift the anchovies out of the lemon juice – they will look pale and 'cooked'. Arrange them on a serving dish. Sprinkle with the spring onions, parsley and a large quantity of olive oil, season with salt and pepper and serve at room temperature.

The combination of sweet, salty Parma ham or a local *prosciutto crudo* and a yielding soft fruit like ripe figs or melon is one of life's little miracles. This is an all-time classic, and none the worse for that. I have been served this with a trickle of aged balsamic vinegar over the figs, which was amazing. If you find a really aged one on your travels, buy it – never mind the expense. It will be thick, sweet and syrupy, and heaven to use in tiny amounts.

parma ham
with figs and balsamic dressing

4 large or 8 small fresh ripe figs (preferably purple ones)

1 tablespoon good balsamic vinegar

extra virgin olive oil, for brushing and serving

12 thin slices of Parma ham or *prosciutto crudo*

150 g fresh Parmesan cheese, broken into craggy lumps

crushed black pepper, to serve

serves 4

Take each fig and stand it upright. Using a sharp knife, make 2 cuts across each fig not quite quartering it, but keeping it intact. Ease the figs open and brush with balsamic vinegar and olive oil.

Arrange 3 slices of Parma ham on each plate with the figs and Parmesan on top. Sprinkle with extra virgin olive oil and plenty of crushed black pepper and serve.

A wonderful explosion of the flavours of sage and anchovy through crisp batter. These must be served virtually straight out of the pan. I sometimes like to use a packet of Japanese tempura batter for this – it is so light and crisp.

deep-fried sage leaves

24 large sage leaves
1 teaspoon salted capers, rinsed
1 tablespoon anchovy paste
vegetable oil, for deep-frying

batter
1 egg
150 ml iced water
125 g plain flour

makes 12

Wash and dry the sage leaves. Mash the capers with the anchovy paste and spread onto the darker green sides of 12 of the leaves. Press another leaf on top of the filling to form a sandwich.

To make the batter, lightly whisk the egg and the iced water together. Add the flour and whisk again, leaving the mixture a bit lumpy. Do not let it stand.

Heat the oil in a deep pan or wok until a piece of stale bread turns golden in a few seconds when dropped in. Holding the leaves by the stems, dip them into the batter and lightly shake off the excess. Place into the hot oil, a few at a time, and fry until crisp and barely golden. This will only take a few seconds. Drain on kitchen paper and serve immediately.

These are a great example of Sicilian street food – little fritters made out of ground chickpeas. So popular throughout the Mediterranean, every country has a form of snack made with these versatile legumes. The fritters are crisp on the outside and soft in the middle. To taste their best, they must be served hot and sprinkled with lots of sea salt.

sicilian chickpea and rosemary fritters

300 g chickpea flour*

750 ml water

1–2 tablespoons chopped fresh rosemary

vegetable oil, for deep-frying

sea salt and freshly ground black pepper

makes about 40

Chickpea flour is known as gram flour in Asian shops

Lightly oil a cold surface such as a marble slab or the back of a large baking sheet. Have a spatula at the ready! Sift the chickpea flour into a saucepan. Whisk in the water slowly, making sure there are no lumps. Stir in the rosemary, and salt and pepper to taste. Bring to the boil, beating all the time, until the mixture really thickens and leaves the side of the pan (like choux pastry). Don't worry if you get lumps at this stage, they will disappear when you fry the fritters.

Now you need to work really quickly. Tip the mixture onto the oiled surface and spread it out as thinly and evenly as you can – aim to make it about 3 mm thick. Let cool and set.

When set, cut into small triangles or squares. To prevent them drying out, place them between layers of plastic kitchen wrap until ready to cook. Heat some oil in a wok or deep-fryer – the oil is at the correct temperature when a piece of mixture will sizzle instantly when dropped in. Deep-fry a few fritters at a time, turning when golden brown. Drain on kitchen paper and sprinkle with salt. Serve hot.

traditional peasant tomato and garlic bruschetta

This is called *fettunta* in Italy, a word that comes from the Tuscan dialect and derives from Latin, meaning 'anointed slice'. It is a slice of bread grilled over hot coals, rubbed with garlic and drizzled with olive oil. To be authentic, you should use only the finest Tuscan extra virgin olive oil. The ripe tomato is just crushed in your hand and smashed onto the bread, then eaten immediately. This is bruschetta at its simplest and best. Here is a more civilized version, but you should try the real thing.

Roughly chop the tomatoes and season with salt and pepper.

To make the bruschetta, grill, toast or pan-grill the bread on both sides until lightly charred or toasted. Rub the top side of each slice with the cut garlic, then drizzle with olive oil.

Spoon the tomatoes over the bruschetta and drizzle with more olive oil. Eat immediately with your fingers.

4 large very ripe tomatoes

4 thick slices of country bread, preferably sourdough

2 garlic cloves, halved

extra virgin olive oil, for drizzling

sea salt and freshly ground black pepper

serves 4

This is pared-down simplicity and so easy to make. It beats the likes of doughballs and garlic bread hands down. The most important thing is not to overcook the garlic – it must on no account turn brown. This is great served instead of garlic bread with a selection of salads.

olive oil and garlic bruschetta

Cut the garlic lengthways into paper-thin slices. Heat the olive oil in a small saucepan and stir in the garlic. Cook until the garlic starts to give off its aroma and is golden but not brown (or it will taste bitter). Remove the pan from the heat, then mix in the chilli flakes and parsley, if using. Cover to keep warm.

To make the bruschetta, grill, toast or pan-grill the bread on both sides until lightly charred or toasted. Spoon or brush over the garlicky chilli oil. Eat immediately with your fingers!

4 large garlic cloves

6 tablespoons extra virgin olive oil

a good pinch of dried chilli flakes

4 tablespoons chopped fresh parsley (optional)

bruschetta

4 thick slices of country bread, preferably sourdough

extra virgin olive oil, for drizzling

serves 4

artichoke, pesto and pine nut bruschetta

This is a joy to make when fresh artichokes are in season. The pesto and pine nuts are perfect foils for the slightly bitter taste of the artichoke. If fresh ones are unavailable, use canned artichokes or those preserved in oil. Whichever you use, lightly fry them to bring out their full flavour.

To make the bruschetta, grill, toast or pan-grill the bread on both sides until lightly charred or toasted. Rub the top side of each slice with the cut garlic, then drizzle with olive oil. Keep them warm in a low oven.

Prepare the artichokes* and cut them in half. Heat the oil and butter in a frying pan, add the artichokes and fry gently until they are completely tender and beginning to brown. Add the balsamic vinegar, turn up the heat and toss the artichokes until the vinegar evaporates.

To make the pesto Genovese, put the garlic, pine nuts, grated Parmesan, basil leaves, olive oil and salt and pepper in a blender or food processor and blend until smooth.

Spread the pesto over the bruschetta and divide the artichokes between the slices. Scatter with the pine nuts and Parmesan shavings. Serve immediately.

*Note To prepare fresh artichokes, fill a large bowl with water and squeeze in the juice of ½ lemon. Use the other lemon half to rub the cut portions of the artichokes as you work. Trim the artichokes by snapping off the dark green outer leaves, starting at the base. Trim the stalk to about 5 cm and peel the fibrous outside of the stalk with a vegetable peeler. Cut about 1 cm off the tip of each artichoke, then put them in the lemony water, to stop them discolouring, until required.

4 thick slices of country bread, preferably sourdough

2 garlic cloves, halved

extra virgin olive oil, for brushing

artichoke topping

6 small, fresh artichokes, each about 8 cm long

2 tablespoons olive oil

25 g butter

1 tablespoon balsamic vinegar

pesto genovese

2 garlic cloves

50 g pine nuts

4 tablespoons freshly grated Parmesan cheese

50 g fresh basil leaves

150 ml extra virgin olive oil

sea salt and freshly ground black pepper

to serve

2 tablespoons pine nuts, toasted

shavings of Parmesan cheese

serves 4

This is a very popular combination of ingredients in southern Italy. Sweet prawns and tomatoes contrast with earthy chickpeas, pungent garlic and a hint of fiery chilli. Great food for warm summer evenings in the garden.

spicy garlic prawns *with tomatoes and chickpeas on bruschetta*

Heat the oil in a large frying pan and add the garlic, fry until just turning golden (do not let it burn), then add the chilli and wine. Turn up the heat and boil fast to reduce the wine to almost nothing. Add the tomatoes (if you are using canned tomatoes add some sugar to bring out their flavour) and cook for 1–2 minutes until they start to soften. Stir in the prawns and chickpeas and bring to the boil. Simmer for 2–3 minutes, then stir in the parsley and season with salt and pepper to taste. Set aside.

To make the bruschetta, grill, toast or pan grill the bread on both sides until lightly charred or toasted. Rub the top side of each slice with the cut garlic, then drizzle with olive oil. Spoon over the prawn mixture and serve immediately.

2 tablespoons extra virgin olive oil, plus extra for drizzling

2 garlic cloves, finely chopped

1/2 teaspoon dried chilli flakes

100 ml dry white wine

250 g ripe tomatoes, peeled and chopped, or canned tomatoes, chopped

1/2 teaspoon sugar (optional)

200 g raw, shelled prawns

4 tablespoons canned chickpeas, rinsed and drained

2 tablespoons chopped fresh flat leaf parsley

4 thick slices of country bread, preferably sourdough

2 garlic cloves, halved

sea salt and freshly ground black pepper

serves 4

grilled fig and prosciutto bruschetta
with rocket

4 thick slices of country bread, preferably sourdough

2 garlic cloves, halved

extra virgin olive oil, for drizzling and brushing

8 ripe fresh figs

2 tablespoons balsamic vinegar

12 slices of prosciutto

100 g rocket

sea salt and freshly ground black pepper

shavings of Parmesan cheese, to serve

serves 4

This combination of caramelized figs and crisply barbecued prosciutto is irresistible. The figs are best cooked on a barbecue, but you can use a stove-top grill pan or a grill – just get the right amount of charring on the figs.

To make the bruschetta, grill, toast or pan-grill the bread on both sides until lightly charred or toasted. Rub the top side of each slice with the cut garlic, then drizzle with olive oil. Keep them warm in a low oven.

Take the figs and stand them upright. Using a small, sharp knife, make two cuts across each fig not quite quartering it, but keeping it intact at the base. Ease the figs open and brush with balsamic vinegar and olive oil. Put the figs cut side down on a preheated barbecue or stove-top grill pan and cook for 3–4 minutes until hot and slightly charred – don't move them during cooking. Alternatively, put the figs cut side up under a really hot grill until beginning to brown and heated through.

While the figs are cooking, put half the slices of prosciutto on the barbecue or stove-top grill pan, or under the grill and cook until frazzled. Remove and keep warm while cooking the remaining slices. Put two figs, three pieces of prosciutto and some rocket on each slice of bruschetta. Sprinkle with Parmesan shavings and drizzle with olive oil. Season to taste with salt and pepper and serve immediately.

mozzarella in carrozza

This is a classic Italian restaurant favourite, but this more rustic version is so easy to make at home. The mozzarella melts inside the crisp bread coat, revealing a surprise of sun-dried tomatoes and anchovies inside.

2 mozzarella cheeses, thickly sliced

8 thin oval slices of country bread

8 sun-dried tomatoes, soaked until soft and cut into strips

8 anchovy fillets in oil, drained

2 teaspoons dried oregano

3 eggs, beaten

vegetable oil, for shallow frying

sea salt and freshly ground black pepper

serves 4

Arrange the mozzarella slices over 4 of the slices of bread. Scatter the sun-dried tomatoes, anchovy fillets and oregano over the mozzarella. Season well with salt and pepper, then put the remaining bread slices on top to make sandwiches. Press down well.

Pour the beaten eggs into a large dish and dip the sandwiches in them, turning once to coat both sides. Leave them in the egg for 30 minutes to soak it up.

Heat the oil in a deep frying pan until a breadcrumb dropped in sizzles instantly. Fry each sandwich for 1–2 minutes on each side until crisp and golden. Drain on kitchen paper and serve piping hot.

soup

Pappa al pomodoro is only as good as its ingredients – great tomatoes, good bread and wonderful, green (preferably Tuscan) olive oil. This is one of the most comforting soups on earth and of course has its origins in peasant thrift. Leftover bread is never thrown away in Tuscany – there is always a use for it. Here, it thickens a rich tomato soup, which is in turn enriched with Parmesan.

creamy tomato and bread soup *with basil oil*

1.5 litres chicken, meat or Vegetable Stock (page 234)

4 tablespoons olive oil

1 onion, chopped

1.25 kg very ripe, soft tomatoes, coarsely chopped

300 g stale white bread, thinly sliced, crusts removed (or breadcrumbs)

3 garlic cloves, crushed

125 g freshly grated Parmesan cheese, plus extra to serve

sea salt and freshly ground black pepper

basil oil

6 tablespoons chopped fresh basil leaves

150 ml extra virgin olive oil

serves 6

Heat the stock slowly in a large saucepan. Meanwhile, heat the oil in a second large saucepan, add the onion and tomatoes and fry over gentle heat for about 10 minutes until soft. Push the mixture through a food mill, mouli or sieve, and stir into the hot broth. Add the bread and garlic.

Cover and simmer gently for about 45 minutes until thick and creamy, whisking from time to time to break up the bread. Take care, because this soup can catch on the bottom.

Meanwhile, to make the basil oil, put the basil and olive oil in a blender and blend until completely smooth – if not, pour through a fine strainer.

To finish, stir the Parmesan into the soup, then add salt and pepper to taste. Ladle into bowls and trickle 2 tablespoons of basil oil over each serving. Serve hot, warm or cold (but never chilled), with more Parmesan served separately to sprinkle over.

la ribollita

250 g dried cannellini beans

150 ml extra virgin olive oil, plus extra to serve

1 onion, finely chopped

1 carrot, chopped

1 celery stalk, chopped

2 leeks, finely chopped

4 garlic cloves, finely chopped, plus 1 extra peeled and bruised, for rubbing

1 small white cabbage, thinly sliced

1 large potato, chopped

4 medium courgettes, chopped

400 ml tomato passata (strained, crushed tomatoes)

2 sprigs of rosemary

2 sprigs of thyme

2 sprigs of sage

1 dried red chilli

500 g *cavolo nero* (Tuscan black cabbage) or Savoy cabbage, thinly sliced

6 thick slices of coarse crusty white bread

sea salt and freshly ground black pepper

freshly grated Parmesan cheese, to serve

serves 8 generously

There's nothing quite like a huge plate of thick, warming *ribollita* on a damp autumn evening beside a crackling, scented log fire. Best made in large quantities, this is a great soup for a family get-together and is very filling. *Ribollita* means 'reboiled', and is made from whatever vegetables are around, but must contain beans and the Tuscan black winter cabbage, *cavolo nero*. The basic bean and vegetable soup is made the day before, then reheated and ladled over toasted garlic bread, sprinkled with olive oil and served with lots of Parmesan cheese.

Put the beans in a bowl, cover with cold water, soak overnight, then drain just before you're ready to use them.

Next day, heat half the olive oil in a large, heavy stockpot and add the onion, carrot and celery. Cook gently for 10 minutes, stirring frequently. Add the leeks and garlic and cook for another 10 minutes. Add the white cabbage, potato and courgettes, stir well and cook for 10 minutes more, stirring frequently.

Stir in the soaked beans, passata, rosemary, thyme, sage, dried chilli, salt and plenty of black pepper. Cover with about 2 litres of water (the vegetables should be well covered), bring to the boil, then turn down the heat and simmer, covered, for at least 2 hours, until the beans are very soft.

Take out 2–3 large ladles of soup and mash well. Stir back into the soup to thicken it. Stir in the *cavolo nero* or Savoy cabbage and simmer for another 15 minutes.

Remove from the heat, let cool, then refrigerate overnight. The next day, slowly reheat the soup and stir in the remaining olive oil. Toast the bread and rub with garlic. Pile the bread in a tureen or in individual bowls and ladle the soup over the top. Trickle in more olive oil and serve with plenty of freshly grated Parmesan.

spinach broth *with egg and cheese*

700 g fresh spinach

50 g butter

4 eggs

5 tablespoons freshly grated Parmesan cheese

¼ teaspoon freshly grated nutmeg

about 1.75 litres really good chicken stock

sea salt and freshly ground black pepper

serves 6

A typical way to thicken and enrich a broth in many parts of Italy is to add beaten eggs. This is one of the best I have tasted because of the freshness of the greens. Although most of us are limited to spinach, there are many more varieties of *ortaggi* (greens) in Italian markets and greengrocers – beetroot tops, for example, or even courgette leaves and tendrils.

Remove all the stalks from the spinach, then wash the leaves thoroughly – do not shake dry. Cook the leaves in a large saucepan with the water still clinging. When the leaves have wilted, drain well, then chop finely.

Heat the butter in a medium saucepan, then add the spinach, tossing well to coat with the butter. Remove from the heat and let cool for 5 minutes.

Put the eggs, Parmesan, nutmeg, salt and pepper in a bowl and beat well. Mix into the spinach. Put the stock in a large saucepan and bring almost to the boil. When almost boiling, whisk in the spinach and egg mixture as quickly as you can to avoid it curdling. Reheat the soup gently for a couple of minutes, but don't let it boil. Serve immediately.

A lovely soup to serve in the summer when fresh peas and mint are plentiful. *Vialone nano* is the favourite risotto rice in the Veneto region. It is a *semi-fino* round grain rice, best for soups and risotto, but arborio (a *superfino* used mainly for risotto) will do very nicely. This dish has very ancient roots, and was flavoured with fennel seeds at one time. Parsley is the usual addition now, but I prefer mint in the summer.

venetian pea and rice soup *with mint*

Put the stock in a large saucepan and bring it slowly to the boil while you prepare the *soffrito* (sautéed sauce).

Heat the olive oil and half of the butter in a large saucepan and, when melted, add the pancetta and spring onion. Cook for about 5 minutes until softened but not browned.

Pour in the rice, stir for a few minutes to toast it, then add the hot stock. Simmer for 10 minutes, stirring from time to time. Add the peas, cook for another 5–7 minutes, then stir in the remaining butter, mint and Parmesan. Add salt and pepper to taste and serve immediately. The rice grains should not be too mushy, and the soup should be thick, but not stodgy.

1.25 litres chicken, beef or Vegetable Stock (page 234)

2 tablespoons olive oil

60 g butter

50 g pancetta, finely chopped

1 large spring onion (*cipolloto*) or the white parts of 4 spring onions, finely chopped

200 g risotto rice, preferably *vialone nano*

1 kg fresh peas in the pod, shelled, or 400 g frozen peas

3 tablespoons chopped fresh mint leaves

freshly grated Parmesan cheese

sea salt and freshly ground black pepper

serves 4

Italy produces the most wonderful, comforting soups and this one from Campania combines two of the great stand-bys – beans and pasta. This one is sure to bring a smile of nostalgia to the face of any homesick Italian, probably because it will remind them of *nonna's* version.

pasta and bean soup

185 g dried cannellini or haricot beans

a pinch of bicarbonate of soda

4 tablespoons olive oil, plus extra to serve

2 garlic cloves, crushed

1.75 litres chicken stock or water

100 g short pasta shapes, such as *maccheroni* or *tubetti*

4 tomatoes, skinned, deseeded and coarsely chopped

4 tablespoons chopped fresh flat leaf parsley

sea salt and freshly ground black pepper

serves 6

Put the beans in a bowl, cover with cold water, add a pinch of bicarbonate of soda and soak overnight. The next day, drain the beans just before you're ready to use them.

Put the drained beans in a large saucepan. Add the olive oil, garlic and stock or water. Bring to the boil, reduce the heat and simmer, part-covered with a lid, for 1–2 hours or until the beans are tender.

Working in batches if necessary, put the beans and the cooking liquid in a blender or food processor and blend to a purée. Return the bean purée to the rinsed pan, adding extra water or stock if the purée is too thick. Add the pasta to the pan and simmer gently for 15 minutes until tender. (Add a little extra water or stock if the soup is looking too thick.) Stir in the tomatoes and parsley and season well with salt and pepper. Serve the soup with an extra trickle of olive oil.

risotto

When you have nothing except risotto rice in the cupboard, and a chunk of Parmesan and some butter in the refrigerator, yet feel the need for comfort and luxury, this is the risotto for you. It is pale, golden, smooth and creamy and relies totally on the quality of these few ingredients. I would use real sweet, nutty Parmigiano Reggiano and nothing else.

parmesan and butter risotto

about 1.5 litres hot chicken stock or Vegetable Stock (page 234)

150 g unsalted butter

1 onion, finely chopped

500 g risotto rice, preferably *carnaroli*

150 ml dry white wine

100 g freshly grated Parmesan cheese

sea salt and freshly ground black pepper

serves 4–6

Put the stock in a saucepan and keep it at a gentle simmer. Melt half the butter in a large, heavy saucepan and add the onion. Cook gently for 10 minutes until soft, golden and translucent but not browned. Add the rice and stir until well coated with the butter and heated through. Pour in the wine and boil hard until it has reduced and almost disappeared. This will remove the taste of raw alcohol.

Begin adding the stock, a large ladle at a time, stirring gently until each ladle has been almost absorbed by the rice. The risotto should be kept at a bare simmer throughout cooking, so don't let the rice dry out – add more stock as necessary. Continue until the rice is tender and creamy, but the grains still firm. (This should take 15–20 minutes depending on the type of rice used – check the packet instructions.)

Taste and season well with salt and pepper, then stir in the remaining butter and all the Parmesan. Cover and let rest for a couple of minutes so the risotto can relax and the cheese melt, then serve immediately. You may like to add a little more stock just before you serve, but don't let the risotto wait around too long or the rice will turn mushy.

When you dip your fork into this risotto, you will find pockets of melting mozzarella. Mix in the tomato topping and you will make more strings. Try to use *mozzarella di bufala* — made from the milk of buffalos, not cows – which has a fresh, lactic bite, well-suited to this recipe.

mozzarella and sun-blushed
tomato risotto *with basil*

about 1.5 litres hot chicken stock or Vegetable Stock (page 234)

125 g unsalted butter

1 onion, finely chopped

400 g risotto rice

150 ml dry white wine

250 g mozzarella cheese, cut into 1 cm cubes

4 tablespoons chopped fresh basil leaves, plus extra basil leaves to serve (optional)

300 g sun-blushed tomatoes

sea salt and freshly ground black pepper

freshly grated Parmesan cheese, to serve

serves 4

Put the stock in a saucepan and keep it at a gentle simmer. Melt half the butter in a large, heavy saucepan and add the onion. Cook gently for 10 minutes until soft, golden and translucent but not browned. Add the rice and stir until well coated with the butter and heated through. Pour in the wine and boil hard until it has reduced and almost disappeared. This will remove the taste of raw alcohol.

Begin adding the stock, a large ladle at a time, stirring gently until each ladle has been almost absorbed by the rice. The risotto should be kept at a bare simmer throughout cooking, so don't let the rice dry out – add more stock as necessary. Continue until the rice is tender and creamy, but the grains still firm. (This should take 15–20 minutes depending on the type of rice used – check the packet instructions.)

Taste and season well with salt and pepper, then stir in the remaining butter. You may like to add a little more hot stock to loosen the risotto. Fold in the mozzarella and basil. Cover and let rest for a couple of minutes so the risotto can relax and the cheese melt. Ladle into warm bowls and put a pile of tomatoes in the centre of each one. Top with extra basil leaves, if using, and serve immediately with grated Parmesan.

wild mushroom risotto

1.5 litres hot chicken stock or
Vegetable Stock (page 234)

125 g unsalted butter

1 large onion, finely chopped

2 garlic cloves, finely chopped

250 g mixed wild mushrooms, cleaned
and coarsely chopped (or a mixture of
wild and fresh, or 200 g cultivated
mushrooms, plus 25 g dried porcini
soaked in warm water for 20 minutes,
drained and chopped)

1 tablespoon each of chopped fresh
thyme and marjoram

150 ml dry white wine or vermouth

500 g risotto rice

75 g freshly grated Parmesan cheese,
plus extra to serve

sea salt and freshly ground
black pepper

serves 6

We make this risotto in our cooking classes in Tuscany in October when fresh porcini mushrooms are around. Any fresh wild mushroom will taste wonderful – chanterelles, girolles or black *trompettes de mort*. However, it can be made very successfully using a mixture of cultivated mushrooms and dried reconstituted porcini.

Put the stock in a saucepan and keep it at a gentle simmer. Melt the butter in a large, heavy saucepan and add the onion and garlic. Cook gently for 10 minutes until soft, golden and translucent but not browned. Stir in the mushrooms and herbs, then cook over medium heat for 3 minutes to heat through. Pour in the wine and boil hard until it has reduced and almost disappeared. This will remove the taste of raw alcohol. Stir in the rice and fry until dry and slightly opaque.

Begin adding the stock, a large ladle at a time, stirring gently until each ladle has been almost absorbed by the rice. The risotto should be kept at a bare simmer throughout cooking, so don't let the rice dry out – add more stock as necessary. Continue until the rice is tender and creamy, but the grains still firm. (This should take 15–20 minutes depending on the type of rice used – check the packet instructions.)

Taste and season well with salt and pepper. Stir in the Parmesan, cover and let rest for a couple of minutes. Carefully ladle into warm bowls and serve immediately with extra grated Parmesan.

about 1.5 litres hot chicken
stock or Vegetable Stock
(page 234)

125 g unsalted butter

6 spring onions,
finely chopped

2 garlic cloves,
finely chopped

150 g carrots, cubed, or a
bunch of tiny new carrots,
trimmed and scraped but
kept whole

400 g risotto rice,
preferably *carnaroli*

100 g asparagus spears,
trimmed and cut into
2 cm lengths

100 g fine green beans,
cut into 2 cm lengths

100 g fresh or frozen peas
or broad beans, thawed
if frozen

50 g freshly grated
Parmesan cheese,
plus extra to serve

6 tablespoons chopped
mixed fresh herbs, such as
chives, dill, flat leaf parsley,
mint, chervil and tarragon

sea salt and freshly ground
black pepper

serves 4

The charm of this risotto is found in the delicate flavours
and colours of spring. The vegetables are small and sweet,
the herbs fresh and fragrant. Don't be tempted to skimp
on the herbs here – as well as imparting intense flavour,
they add a beautiful touch of spring green. Sometimes
I blend them with the remaining butter (melted) to give
a bright green liquid to beat in at the end.

spring risotto *with herbs*

Put the stock in a saucepan and keep it at a gentle simmer. Melt half
the butter in a large, heavy saucepan and add the spring onions, garlic
and carrots. Cook gently for 5 minutes until the onions are soft and
translucent but not browned. Stir in the rice until well coated with the
butter and heated through.

Begin adding the stock, a large ladle at a time, stirring gently until each
ladle has been almost absorbed by the rice. The risotto should be kept
at a bare simmer throughout cooking, so don't let the rice dry out – add
more stock as necessary. After 10 minutes, add the asparagus, beans
and peas and continue cooking and adding stock until the vegetables
are tender and the rice is tender and creamy, but the grains still firm.
(This should take 15–20 minutes depending on the type of rice used –
check the packet instructions.)

Taste and season well with salt and pepper and stir in the remaining
butter, the Parmesan and the herbs. Cover and let rest for a couple of
minutes, then serve immediately with extra freshly grated Parmesan
cheese. You may like to add a little more hot stock to the risotto just
before you serve to loosen it, but don't let it wait around too long or
the rice will turn mushy.

A dish from the Veneto, where *vialone nano* rice is grown, as well as several varieties of radicchio. Stirring in a spoonful of mascarpone or cream at the end enriches the risotto and adds sweetness. The risotto has both a sweet and a bitter flavour. I like to add a few currants plumped up for 20 minutes in warm grappa for an added surprise.

creamy radicchio
and mascarpone risotto

about 1.5 litres hot chicken stock or Vegetable Stock (page 234)

125 g unsalted butter

2 carrots, finely chopped

125 g smoked pancetta, finely chopped

2 garlic cloves, finely chopped

500 g radicchio, finely shredded

500 g risotto rice

2 tablespoons currants soaked in 4 tablespoons warm grappa for 20 minutes (optional)

3 tablespoons mascarpone cheese or double cream

75 g freshly grated Parmesan cheese, plus extra to serve

sea salt and freshly ground black pepper

serves 6

Put the stock in a saucepan and keep it at a gentle simmer. Melt half the butter in a large, heavy saucepan and add the carrots. Cook gently for 5 minutes until softening. Add the pancetta and garlic, and cook for 4 minutes until just beginning to colour. Stir in the radicchio and cook for 5 minutes until it begins to wilt. Add the rice and stir until heated through.

Begin adding the stock, a large ladle at a time, stirring gently until each ladle has been almost absorbed by the rice. The risotto should be kept at a bare simmer throughout cooking, so don't let the rice dry out – add more stock as necessary. Continue until the rice is tender and creamy, but the grains still firm. (This should take 15–20 minutes depending on the type of rice used – check the packet instructions.)

Taste and season well with salt and plenty of black pepper. Add the soaked currants, if using, and stir in the remaining butter, the mascarpone or cream and the Parmesan. Cover and let rest for a couple of minutes, then serve immediately with extra grated Parmesan.

An amazing risotto to serve on its own as a first course or to accompany meat or game dishes. This risotto needs the sweetness of the vegetables to balance the acidity from the wine. Use a good wine that you would not be ashamed to drink, and you will achieve perfect results. Use a cheap, undrinkable wine and the risotto will be inedible.

red wine risotto

about 1.5 litres chicken stock or Vegetable Stock (page 234)

125 g unsalted butter

1 small red onion, finely chopped

1 small carrot, finely chopped

1 small celery stalk, finely chopped

50 g pancetta, finely chopped (optional)

500 g risotto rice

300 ml full-bodied red wine such as Barolo

125 g freshly grated Parmesan cheese

sea salt and freshly ground black pepper

chopped fresh parsley, to serve

serves 4–6

Put the stock in a saucepan and keep it at a gentle simmer. Melt half the butter in a large, heavy saucepan and add the onion, carrot and celery. Cook gently for 10 minutes until soft, golden and translucent but not browned. Add the pancetta, if using, and cook for another 2 minutes. Add the rice and stir until well coated with the butter and heated through. Pour in the wine and boil hard until it has been reduced by half. This will remove the taste of raw alcohol.

Begin adding the stock, a large ladle at a time, stirring gently until each ladle has been almost absorbed by the rice. The risotto should be kept at a bare simmer throughout cooking, so don't let the rice dry out – add more stock as necessary. Continue until the rice is tender and creamy, but the grains still firm. (This should take 15–20 minutes depending on the type of rice used – check the packet instructions.)

Taste and season well with salt and pepper and stir in the remaining butter and all the Parmesan. Cover and let rest for a couple of minutes so the risotto can relax, then serve immediately, sprinkled with parsley. You may like to add a little more hot stock to the risotto just before you serve to loosen it, but don't let it wait around too long or the rice will turn mushy.

Central and northern Italy are the places to go for good risotto – I've never eaten a good one in the south. Seafood risotto should be creamy and slightly soupy. Generally, you will never be offered Parmesan with a fish risotto (except perhaps squid ink risotto) – it is frowned upon, so don't ask!

seafood and saffron risotto

1 packet of saffron threads

1.5 litres light fish stock

300 ml dry white wine

350 g raw shell-on prawn tails

6 baby squid, cleaned and cut into rings

6 fresh scallops, halved horizontally if large

500 g fresh mussels, cleaned

250 g fresh baby clams (*vongole*) or cockles, rinsed

3 tablespoons olive oil

1 onion, finely chopped

500 g risotto rice

sea salt and freshly ground black pepper

3 tablespoons chopped fresh flat leaf parsley, to serve

serves 6

Put the saffron in a small bowl and cover with boiling water. Set aside to infuse while you cook the fish. Pour the stock and wine into a saucepan and heat to simmering point. Add the prawns and cook for 2 minutes. Add the squid and scallops and cook for a further 2 minutes. Remove all the seafood with a slotted spoon and set aside.

Add the mussels and clams to the stock and bring to the boil. Cover and cook for 3–5 minutes or until all the shells have opened. Remove them with a slotted spoon and set aside. Discard any that haven't opened. Keep the stock at a gentle simmer.

Heat the oil in a large, heavy saucepan and add the onion. Cook gently for 10 minutes until the onion is soft and translucent but not browned. Stir in the rice until well coated with the oil and heated through.

Begin adding the hot stock, a large ladle at a time, stirring gently until each ladle has been almost absorbed by the rice. Add the saffron water with the first ladle. The risotto should be kept at a bare simmer throughout cooking, so don't let the rice dry out – add more stock as necessary. Continue adding the stock, ladle by ladle, until all but 2 ladles of stock remain, and the rice is tender and creamy, but the grains still firm. (This should take 15–20 minutes depending on the type of rice used – check the packet instructions.) Taste and season well with salt and pepper.

Finally, stir in the remaining stock and seafood, cover and let stand for 5 minutes. Transfer to a large warmed bowl and sprinkle with parsley. Serve immediately.

My favourite cultivated mushrooms are the large, flat, open, almost black portobellos. They have much more flavour than younger ones with closed caps, and are the next best thing to wild mushrooms. They absorb a lot of butter and I like to get them really brown to concentrate the flavour. Tarragon goes particularly well with this combination, but don't use too much.

chicken and mushroom risotto *with tarragon*

250 g large portobello mushrooms

150 g unsalted butter

1 garlic clove, finely chopped

about 1.5 litres hot chicken stock

1 onion, finely chopped

1 celery stalk, finely chopped

600 g boneless, skinless chicken thighs and breast, finely chopped

500 g risotto rice

300 ml dry white wine

2 teaspoons chopped fresh tarragon

75 g freshly grated Parmesan cheese

sea salt and freshly ground black pepper

chopped fresh parsley, to serve

serves 6

To prepare the mushrooms, cut them into long slices. Melt half the butter in a frying pan, add the mushrooms and garlic and fry over medium heat until browning at the edges. Transfer to a plate and set aside.

Put the stock in a saucepan and keep it at a gentle simmer. Melt half the remaining butter in a large, heavy saucepan and add the onion and celery. Cook gently for 10 minutes until soft and translucent but not browned. Add the chicken and cook for another 5 minutes, but do not let it colour and harden. Add the rice and stir until well coated with butter, heated through and beginning to smell 'toasted'. Pour in the wine, bring to the boil and boil hard to reduce by half – this will concentrate the flavour and remove the taste of raw alcohol.

Begin adding the stock, a large ladle at a time, stirring gently until each ladle has been almost absorbed by the rice. The risotto should be kept at a bare simmer throughout cooking, so don't let the rice dry out – add more stock as necessary. Continue in this way until the rice is tender and creamy, but the grains still firm. (This should take 15–20 minutes depending on the type of rice used – check the packet instructions.)

Taste and season well with salt and pepper and stir in the remaining butter, the tarragon and Parmesan. Cover and let rest for a couple of minutes. Reheat the mushrooms, then serve the risotto with the mushrooms piled on top and sprinkled with chopped parsley.

ham and leek risotto

The leek is one of my favourite vegetables – it's not used enough in my opinion. Its sweet, delicate onion flavour is an excellent complement to salty cooked ham. Try to find ham sold in the piece so you can tear it into shreds – it will be more succulent than sliced ham. Roasting garlic softens and mellows the flavour until it is almost nutty.

6 large garlic cloves

about 200 ml olive oil

500 g leeks

about 1.5 litres hot chicken stock

500 g risotto rice

1 tablespoon coarsegrain mustard

350 g cold roasted ham, shredded

50 g freshly grated Parmesan cheese

sea salt and freshly ground black pepper

fried leeks

2 leeks

sunflower oil, for frying

serves 4–6

Peel the garlic cloves and put them in a small saucepan. Cover with olive oil and heat to simmering. Simmer for about 20 minutes or until the garlic is golden and soft. Remove the pan from the heat and let the garlic cool in the oil.

To make the fried leeks, cut the 2 leeks into 7 cm lengths, then slice in half lengthways and cut into long, thin shreds. Fill a wok or large saucepan one-third full with the sunflower oil and heat to 175°C (350°F). Add the shredded leeks and deep-fry for 1 minute until crisp and just golden. Drain on kitchen paper and set aside.

Slice the 500 g leeks (thinly or thickly, as you like) into rounds. Put the stock in a saucepan and keep it at a gentle simmer. Heat 75 ml of the garlic-flavoured olive oil in a large heavy saucepan. Add the leeks and sauté for a few minutes until beginning to soften and colour slightly, then stir in the cooked garlic cloves. Pour in the rice and stir until well coated with oil and heated through.

Begin to add the simmering stock, a large ladle at a time, stirring gently until each ladle has been almost absorbed by the rice. Continue until the rice is tender and creamy, but the grains still firm. (This should take 15–20 minutes depending on the type of rice used – check the packet instructions.) Stir in the mustard and ham, then season well with salt and pepper. Stir in the Parmesan, then cover and let rest for a couple of minutes so the risotto can relax. Serve immediately, topped with a mound of fried leeks.

pasta and polenta

There are many variations of this pasta dish in Sicily. The tomato sauce is very rich, but this is balanced by grated *ricotta salata* – ewe's milk ricotta cheese, salted and aged. It is very dry and concentrated, but sharp and salty. The nearest thing you can find to it outside the area is aged pecorino or even feta cheese.

spaghetti *with aubergine and tomato sauce*

3 medium aubergines

500 g very ripe red tomatoes
(add 2 tablespoons tomato purée
if not red enough)

3 tablespoons olive oil

3 garlic cloves, chopped

350 g spaghetti or spaghettini

vegetable oil, for frying

3 tablespoons chopped
fresh basil leaves

3–4 tablespoons freshly grated
ricotta salata, aged pecorino
or Parmesan cheese,
plus extra to serve

sea salt

serves 4

Cut the aubergines into small dice and put them in a colander. Sprinkle with salt and put the colander on a plate. Set aside to drain for 30 minutes.

Meanwhile, dip the tomatoes in boiling water for 10 seconds, then drop them into cold water. Slip off and discard the skins, cut the tomatoes in half and squeeze out and discard the seeds. Chop the flesh coarsely.

Heat the olive oil in a frying pan, add the garlic and fry for 2–3 minutes until golden. Add the tomatoes and cook for about 15 minutes until the tomatoes start to disintegrate.

Bring a large saucepan of salted water to the boil, add the spaghetti or spaghettini and cook according to the packet instructions, about 8 minutes.

Meanwhile, rinse the aubergines, drain them and pat dry. Heat 3 cm vegetable oil in a frying pan, add the cubes of aubergine and shallow fry until deep golden brown. Remove and drain on kitchen paper. Stir into the tomato sauce.

Drain the pasta, reserving 2 tablespoons of the cooking water in the pan. Return the pasta to the hot pan. Stir in the tomato and aubergine sauce, chopped basil and grated cheese. Serve immediately with more cheese sprinkled on top.

Taleggio is a soft cheese and not easy to slice thinly. A good trick is to freeze the cheese for 10–15 minutes before slicing it. Truffle oil has an earthy, intense flavour that goes beautifully with mushrooms – if you have some, add a couple of drops to the cooked mezzalune.

mushroom mezzalune

2 tablespoons olive oil

1 garlic clove, finely chopped

250 g small chestnut or field mushrooms, sliced

2 tablespoons Marsala or medium sherry

1 quantity Fresh Egg Pasta (page 232)

200 g Taleggio cheese, thinly sliced

6 slices of Parma ham, halved

sea salt and freshly ground black pepper

to serve

truffle oil or olive oil

fresh basil leaves

a round bowl, about 14 cm diameter

serves 4

Heat the oil in a frying pan, add the garlic and cook for 1 minute. Add the mushrooms and salt and pepper to taste and cook for 3–4 minutes until golden. Add the Marsala or sherry, remove from the heat and let cool.

Roll the rested pasta dough into a thin sheet. If you are using a pasta machine, roll to the second to last setting. Put the pasta on a lightly floured work surface. Put the bowl, upside down, on top of the pasta and cut around it with a knife. Repeat to make 12 rounds. Put a slice of Taleggio on one side of each round, spoon over the mushrooms and top with a piece of Parma ham, folded to fit if necessary. Dampen the edges lightly with water and fold each circle over to form a semi-circle, pressing the edges together firmly to enclose the filling and seal.

Bring a large saucepan of salted water to the boil. Add half the mezzalune and cook for 3–4 minutes until they rise to the surface and are cooked through. Drain well and keep them warm while you cook the remaining mezzalune. Divide between 4 bowls or plates, sprinkle with truffle or olive oil, basil leaves and a grinding of black pepper and serve.

Note If you are not cooking the mezzalune immediately, arrange in a single layer on a tray lined with non-stick parchment paper, cover with another sheet of parchment paper and chill for up to 2 hours.

cannelloni *with ricotta, bitter greens and cherry tomato sauce*

12 dried cannelloni tubes,
12 sheets fresh or dried lasagne
or 1 recipe Fresh Egg Pasta
(page 232)

tomato sauce

3 tablespoons olive oil

2 garlic cloves, finely chopped

750 g cherry tomatoes, halved

3 tablespoons chopped fresh
basil leaves

sea salt and freshly ground
black pepper

ricotta filling

100 g bitter salad greens such as
rocket, watercress or spinach

500 g ricotta cheese

2 eggs, beaten

100 g freshly grated
Parmesan cheese

freshly grated nutmeg, to taste

*a piping bag with a large
plain nozzle*

*a shallow ovenproof dish,
buttered*

serves 4–6

This cannelloni combines a creamy sharp ricotta filling, speckled with slightly bitter greens and a sweet tomato sauce. The contrast between the sauce and filling is amazing.

To make the tomato sauce, heat the oil in a saucepan, add the garlic and cook until just turning golden. Add the halved tomatoes. They should hiss as they go in – this will slightly caramelize the juices and concentrate the flavour. Stir well, then simmer for 10 minutes. Stir in the basil and season with salt and pepper (the sauce should still appear quite lumpy). Remove from the heat and set aside.

To make the ricotta filling, plunge the salad greens into a saucepan of boiling water for 1 minute, then drain well, squeezing out any excess moisture. Chop finely. Press the ricotta through a sieve into a bowl. Beat in the eggs, then add the chopped greens and half the Parmesan. Season with nutmeg, salt and pepper. Set aside.

Cook the cannelloni or lasagne sheets in a large saucepan of boiling salted water according to the packet instructions. If using homemade pasta, cook for 1 minute. Lift out of the water and drain on a clean tea towel.

Spoon the ricotta filling into the piping bag. Fill each tube of cannelloni or pipe down the shorter edge of each lasagne sheet and roll it up. Arrange the filled cannelloni tightly together in a single layer in the prepared dish. Spoon over the tomato sauce and sprinkle with the remaining Parmesan. Bake in a preheated oven at 200°C (400°F) Gas 6 for 25–30 minutes until bubbling. Serve immediately.

tomato sauce *with double basil*

3 tablespoons
olive oil

2 garlic cloves,
finely chopped

1 shallot, finely
chopped

25 g fresh basil
leaves

500 g ripe tomatoes,
coarsely chopped,
or 400 g canned
plum tomatoes

a pinch of sugar

350 g dried pasta,
such as spaghetti
or linguine

sea salt and freshly
ground black pepper

freshly grated
Parmesan cheese,
to serve

serves 4

The basil is added in two stages; first for depth of flavour, then at the end for a burst of fresh fragrance – double basil. In summer, use fragrant, ripe tomatoes.

Heat the oil in a saucepan and add the garlic, shallot and half the basil. Cook for 3–4 minutes until the shallot is golden.

Add the tomatoes and cook, stirring, for 10 minutes, until thickened and pulpy. Add the sugar, 100 ml water and salt and pepper to taste. Bring to the boil, cover and simmer very gently for 1 hour until dark red and thickened, with droplets of oil on the surface.

Bring a large saucepan of salted water to the boil. Add the pasta and cook according to the packet instructions, about 8 minutes.

Drain the pasta, reserving 2 tablespoons of the cooking water in the pan. Return the pasta to the hot pan. Tear the remaining basil leaves into the tomato sauce and add the sauce to the pasta. Toss well, sprinkle with the Parmesan and serve.

white spaghetti

This is one of those storecupboard dishes that is great when you get home late, tired and hungry. Keep a stock of anchovies, olive oil, and spaghetti and you can always make this dish at short notice.

Bring a large saucepan of salted water to the boil. Add the pasta and cook according to the packet instructions, about 8 minutes.

Put the olive oil and garlic in a small saucepan and heat very gently over low heat for 4–5 minutes until the garlic is pale golden but not browned. Remove and discard the garlic.

Add the anchovies and 100 ml water to the pan and simmer rapidly, whisking with the fork until the anchovies have almost dissolved. Add plenty of black pepper and a pinch of salt.

Drain the pasta, reserving 2 tablespoons of the cooking water in the pan. Return the pasta to the hot pan. Add the anchovy mixture and toss well. Divide between 2 bowls or plates and serve.

150 g dried spaghetti

6 tablespoons olive oil

4 garlic cloves, halved

6 anchovy fillets in oil, drained

sea salt and freshly ground black pepper

serves 2

Puttanesca was famously named in honour of the ladies of the night, although no one seems quite sure why. Maybe it's because the sauce has a wild and fiery character. This robust dish is perfectly matched by a full-bodied red wine.

pasta *with puttanesca sauce*

2 tablespoons olive oil

1 onion, finely chopped

2 garlic cloves, finely chopped

4 anchovy fillets in oil, drained and coarsely chopped

2 red chillies, finely chopped

4 ripe tomatoes, coarsely chopped

1 tablespoon salted capers, well rinsed and coarsely chopped

100 ml red wine

350 g dried pasta, such as gemelli or penne

75 g small black olives

2 tablespoons chopped fresh flat leaf parsley

sea salt freshly ground black pepper

freshly grated Parmesan cheese, to serve

serves 4

Heat the oil in a saucepan, then add the onion, garlic, anchovies and chillies. Cook over medium heat for 4–5 minutes until softened and golden. Add the tomatoes and cook for 3–4 minutes, stirring occasionally, until softened. Add the capers, wine and black pepper to taste, then cover and simmer for 20 minutes.

Meanwhile, bring a large saucepan of salted water to the boil. Add the pasta and cook according to the packet instructions, about 10 minutes.

Drain the pasta, reserving 2 tablespoons of the cooking water in the pan. Return the pasta to the hot pan. Add the tomato sauce, olives and parsley and toss well. Divide between 4 bowls and serve sprinkled with grated Parmesan.

Smoked salmon adds a lovely delicate flavour to this dish. Add it right at the last moment so it doesn't overcook or break into tiny pieces.

creamy smoked salmon sauce

300 g dried pasta, such as fusilli bucati or farfalle

300 ml double cream

2 garlic cloves, crushed

200 g smoked salmon, cut into 1 cm strips

4 tablespoons freshly grated Parmesan cheese, plus extra to serve

sea salt and freshly ground black pepper

2 tablespoons snipped fresh chives, to serve

serves 4

Bring a large saucepan of salted water to the boil. Add the pasta and cook according to the packet instructions.

Meanwhile, put the double cream and garlic in a small saucepan. Add salt and pepper to taste and heat gently until warmed through.

Drain the pasta and return it to the hot pan. Add the hot cream, smoked salmon and Parmesan and toss gently. Divide between 4 bowls or plates, sprinkle with chives and extra Parmesan and serve.

Long pasta is the choice for seafood dishes around coastal Italy – spaghetti and spaghettini in the south. This is a simple dish made with local ingredients – nothing sophisticated, but so good. This dish is equally good made with small clams instead of the mussels.

spaghetti *with mussels, tomatoes and parsley*

1 kg live mussels or
small clams

4 tablespoons olive oil

300 ml dry white wine

500 g spaghetti or
spaghettini

2 garlic cloves, crushed

400 g canned chopped
tomatoes

2 tablespoons chopped
fresh flat leaf parsley

sea salt and freshly ground
black pepper

serves 4

Put the mussels in a bowl of cold water and rinse several times to remove any grit or sand. Pull off the beards and scrub well, discarding any that are not firmly closed. Drain.

Heat the oil and wine in a saucepan and add the mussels. Stir over high heat until the mussels open. Remove and discard any that don't open. Lift out the cooked mussels with a slotted spoon and put them in a bowl. Reserve the cooking liquid.

Bring a large saucepan of salted water to the boil. Add the spaghetti and cook according to the packet instructions, about 8 minutes.

Meanwhile, add the garlic to the mussel cooking liquid in the pan and boil fast to concentrate the flavour. Stir in the tomatoes, return to the boil and boil fast for 3–4 minutes until reduced. Stir in the mussels and half the parsley and heat through. Taste and season well with salt and pepper.

Drain the pasta, reserving 2 tablespoons of the cooking water in the pan. Return the pasta to the hot pan and stir in the sauce. Sprinkle with the remaining parsley and serve.

Note If any of the mussels are open when you buy them, make sure that when you tap each one sharply against the work surface it closes. If it doesn't, it is dead and should be thrown away. It's a good idea to soak the mussels in cold water overnight to purify them before cleaning them.

250 g dried pasta, such as
fusilli or fusilli bucati

1 tablespoon butter

2 plum tomatoes,
coarsely chopped

1 garlic clove,
finely chopped

4 tablespoons chilli vodka

150 ml double cream

sea salt and freshly ground
black pepper

to serve

freshly grated Parmesan
cheese

freshly snipped chives

serves 2

If you haven't got chilli vodka, add a small, finely chopped chilli at the same time as the garlic and use plain vodka.

creamy vodka sauce

Bring a large saucepan of salted water to the boil. Add the pasta and cook according to the packet instructions, about 8 minutes.

Meanwhile, heat the butter in a small saucepan, add the tomatoes and garlic and cook for 3 minutes. Add the vodka and boil rapidly for 2 minutes. Reduce the heat and simmer for 2–3 minutes, then stir in the cream and simmer gently for a further 5 minutes. Add salt and pepper to taste.

Drain the pasta, then return it to the hot pan. Add the creamy sauce and mix well. Transfer to 2 serving bowls, then sprinkle with chives, Parmesan and black pepper and serve.

pasta *with carbonara sauce*

This is traditionally served with spaghetti, but any long or ribbon shape, such as tagliatelle or linguine, will be fine.

Bring a large saucepan of salted water to the boil. Add the pasta and cook according to the packet instructions, about 8 minutes.

Meanwhile, heat the butter in a small frying pan, add the shallot, garlic and bacon and cook for 5 minutes until golden. Put the eggs, cream and Parmesan in a bowl and beat to mix, adding salt and pepper to taste.

Drain the pasta, reserving 2 tablespoons of the cooking water in the pan. Return the pasta to the hot pan, but don't return it to the heat. Add the shallot mixture, then the egg mixture and toss well. Divide between 2 serving bowls, sprinkle with Parmesan and black pepper, then serve.

200 g dried pasta, such as
spaghetti or linguine

1 tablespoon butter

1 shallot, finely chopped

2 garlic cloves,
finely chopped

6 slices of smoked streaky
bacon, chopped

2 eggs

150 ml single cream

2 tablespoons freshly
grated Parmesan cheese,
plus extra to serve

sea salt and freshly ground
black pepper

serves 2

about 12 sheets of dried or fresh *lasagne verdi*, made from Spinach Pasta (page 232) rolled out to the second to last setting on the pasta machine

double recipe Béchamel Sauce (page 229)

about 50 g freshly grated Parmesan cheese

ragù

75 g pancetta or dry-cure smoked bacon in a piece

100 g chicken livers

50 g butter

1 medium onion, finely chopped

1 medium carrot, chopped

1 celery stalk, finely chopped

250 g lean minced beef

2 tablespoons tomato purée

100 ml dry white wine

200 ml beef stock or water

freshly grated nutmeg

sea salt and freshly ground black pepper

a deep baking dish, about 20 x 25 cm, buttered

serves 4–6

The classic version of this dish is pasta layered with meat sauce and creamy *salsa besciamella* (béchamel sauce). It is very easy to assemble. Make the *ragù* the day before, and the *besciamella* on the day. If you use fresh pasta, it doesn't need precooking, and is layered up as it is. Just make sure the meat sauce is quite liquid. This will be absorbed into the pasta as it cooks.

lasagne al forno

To make the ragù, cut the pancetta into small cubes. Trim the chicken livers, removing any fat or gristle. Cut off any discoloured bits, which will be bitter if left on. Coarsely chop the livers.

Melt the butter in a saucepan, add the pancetta and cook for 2–3 minutes until beginning to brown. Add the onion, carrot and celery and brown these too. Stir in the minced beef and brown until just changing colour, but not hardening – break it up with a wooden spoon. Stir in the chicken livers and cook for 2–3 minutes. Add the tomato purée, mix well and pour in the wine and stock. Season well with nutmeg, salt and pepper. Bring to the boil, cover and simmer very gently for as long as you can – ideally 2 hours if possible.

Cook the sheets of dried lasagne in plenty of boiling water in batches according to the packet instructions. Lift out with a slotted spoon and drain on a clean tea towel. Fresh pasta will not need boiling.

Spoon one-third of the meat sauce into a buttered baking dish. Cover with 4 sheets of lasagne and spread with one-third of the béchamel sauce. Repeat twice more, finishing with a layer of béchamel covering the whole top. Sprinkle with Parmesan cheese. Bake in a preheated oven at 180°C (350°F) Gas 4 for about 45 minutes until brown and bubbling. Let stand for 10 minutes to settle and firm up before serving.

Fontina is one of the oldest cheeses made in the Valle d'Aosta. It is rich and nutty and melts very easily. It is also the basis of a type of fondue called *fonduta*. This polenta dish is typical fare in some of the little family restaurants you come across off-piste when skiing in Italy. Just the stuff to keep the cold out and set you on your way.

baked polenta *with fontina and pancetta*

If using instant polenta, cook according to the packet instructions, then turn it out into a mound on a wooden board. Let it cool and set.

If using polenta flour, bring 1 litre salted water to the boil, then slowly sprinkle in the polenta flour through your fingers, whisking all the time to stop lumps forming. Cook, stirring with a wooden spoon, for 45 minutes on low heat and then turn out into a mound on a wooden board and let cool and set.

Meanwhile, slice the fontina thinly or grate it. Cut the polenta into slices about 1 cm thick. Arrange a layer of polenta in the ovenproof dish. Top with half the fontina and half the Parmesan. Season with salt and pepper. Add another layer of polenta, then cover with the remaining fontina and the remaining Parmesan. Finally, add a layer of pancetta.

Bake in a preheated oven at 180°C (350°F) Gas 4 for 40 minutes until brown and bubbling and the pancetta crisping on top. Remove from the oven and serve.

300 g instant polenta or real polenta flour

350 g fontina, raclette, or a mixture of grated mozzarella and Cheddar cheese

100 g freshly grated Parmesan cheese

175 g thinly sliced smoked pancetta

sea salt and freshly ground black pepper

a shallow ovenproof dish, 20 x 25 cm, buttered

serves 6

soft polenta *with sausage ragù*

This is a real winter-warmer from the north of Italy, where polenta is the staple carbohydrate. I have been to a polenta night where the steaming soft cereal was poured straight onto a huge wooden board set in the middle of the table. The sauce was poured into a large hollow in the centre of the polenta and everyone gathered round to help themselves directly from the pile – no plates necessary.

2 teaspoons salt

300 g instant polenta

freshly grated Parmesan cheese, to serve

sausage ragù

500 g fresh Italian pork sausages or good all-meat pork sausages

2 tablespoons olive oil

1 medium onion, finely chopped

500 ml tomato passata (strained crushed tomatoes)

150 ml dry red wine

6 sun-dried tomatoes in oil, drained and sliced

sea salt and freshly ground black pepper

serves 4

To make the ragù, squeeze the sausage meat out of the skins into a bowl and break up the meat. Heat the oil in a medium saucepan and add the onion. Cook for 5 minutes until soft and golden. Stir in the sausage meat, browning it all over and breaking up the lumps with a wooden spoon. Pour in the passata and the wine. Bring to the boil. Add the sun-dried tomatoes, then simmer for 30 minutes or until well reduced, stirring occasionally. Add salt and pepper to taste.

Meanwhile, bring 1.4 litres water to the boil with 2 teaspoons salt. Sprinkle in the polenta, stirring or whisking to prevent lumps forming.

Simmer for 5–10 minutes, stirring constantly, until thickened like soft mashed potato. Quickly spoon the polenta into 4 large, warm soup plates and make a hollow in the centre of each. Top with the sausage ragù and serve sprinkled with grated Parmesan cheese.

A warming winter dish to eat by a roaring fire. This is sublime comfort food, loaded with sausage and strings of melting cheese. If you can't find Italian sausages, choose those with the highest meat content and bags of flavour. At the risk of being sacrilegious, Spanish chorizo would be great in this dish.

polenta baked
with italian sausage and cheese

300 g instant polenta or real polenta flour

500 g fresh Italian pork sausages (or good, all-meat pork sausages)

1 tablespoon olive oil

1 red onion, finely chopped

150 ml meat or Vegetable Stock (page 234)

3 tablespoons mixed chopped fresh rosemary and sage

350 g Taleggio cheese, chopped or grated

160 g freshly grated Parmesan cheese

a few pieces of butter

sea salt and freshly ground black pepper

a shallow ovenproof dish, buttered

serves 6

If using instant polenta, cook according to the packet instructions, then turn it out into a mound on a wooden board. Let it cool and set.

If using polenta flour, bring 1 litre salted water to the boil, then slowly sprinkle in the polenta flour through your fingers, whisking all the time to stop lumps forming. Cook, stirring with a wooden spoon, for 45 minutes on low heat and then turn out into a mound on a wooden board and let it cool and set.

Slice the sausages very thickly. Heat the olive oil in a non-stick frying pan, add the sausages and fry until browned on all sides. Add the onion and cook for 5 minutes until softening. Add the stock, half the chopped herbs and season with salt and pepper.

Cut the polenta into 1.5 cm slices. Arrange a layer of polenta in the prepared dish. Add half the sausage mixture, half the Taleggio and half the Parmesan, in layers. Cover with another layer of polenta, add layers of the remaining sausage mixture, Taleggio and Parmesan and dot with a few pieces of butter. Sprinkle with the remaining herbs.

Bake in a preheated oven at 180°C (350°F) Gas 4 for 40 minutes until brown and bubbling.

Soft and golden, these gnocchi are a staple in the Lazio area around Rome. I have added herbs and mustard to the basic mix and like to serve them with roasted rabbit or lamb.

roman gnocchi *with herbs and semolina*

Pour the milk into a saucepan and whisk in the semolina. Bring slowly to the boil, stirring all the time until it really thickens – about 10 minutes (it should be quite thick, like choux paste). Beat in half the Parmesan, half the butter, the egg yolks, mustard, sage and parsley. Add salt and pepper to taste.

Spread the mixture onto the lined baking sheet to a depth of 1.25 cm. Let cool and set, about 2 hours.

When set, cut into triangles or circles with the biscuit cutter. Spread the trimmings from the chopped gnocchi in the bottom of the ovenproof dish. Dot with some of the remaining butter and sprinkle with a little Parmesan. Arrange the gnocchi shapes in a single layer over the trimmings. Dot with the remaining butter and Parmesan. Bake in a preheated oven at 200°C (400°F) Gas 6 for 20–25 minutes until golden and crusty. Let stand for 5 minutes before serving.

1 litre milk

250 g semolina

175 g freshly grated Parmesan cheese

125 g butter

2 egg yolks

1 tablespoon Dijon mustard

2 tablespoons chopped fresh sage

3 tablespoons chopped fresh flat leaf parsley

sea salt and freshly ground black pepper

a baking sheet lined with clingfilm

a 4.5 cm biscuit cutter

an ovenproof dish, 20 x 25 cm, well buttered

serves 4–6

pizzas, tarts and bread

The secret to a delicious Marinara is in the tomatoes. Choose really ripe, plump varieties. It's well worth the extra effort of skinning and deseeding them – the result is a satin-smooth, fragrant and fruity sauce. Don't be tempted to add any cheese!

marinara pizza

Put a pizza stone or baking sheet in the oven and preheat the oven to 220°C (425°F) Gas 7.

Meanwhile, dip the tomatoes in boiling water for 10 seconds, then drop them into cold water. Slip off and discard the skins, cut the tomatoes in half and squeeze out and discard the seeds. Chop the flesh coarsely.

Heat 2 tablespoons of the oil in a saucepan and add the tomatoes and salt and pepper to taste. Cook for about 5 minutes, stirring occasionally, until thickened and pulpy.

Roll out the dough on a lightly floured work surface to 30 cm diameter and brush with a little oil. Spoon over the tomato sauce and scatter evenly with the garlic and oregano or marjoram. Drizzle over a little more oil.

Carefully transfer the pizza to the hot pizza stone or baking sheet and cook in the preheated oven for 15–20 minutes, until crisp and golden. Serve immediately.

700 g ripe tomatoes

3–4 tablespoons olive oil

1 recipe Basic Pizza Dough (page 231)

3 garlic cloves, very thinly sliced

1 tablespoon chopped fresh oregano or marjoram

sea salt and freshly ground black pepper

a pizza stone or baking sheet

serves 2

The recipe for this pizza dough was given to me by a gravel-voiced *pizzaiolo* in Sicily. He insists that using a touch of lemon juice in the dough makes it light and crisp, and I have to agree. Use ordinary plain flour, if you prefer.

margherita pizza

250 g fine Italian semolina flour (*farina di semola*)

7 g fresh yeast

1 tablespoon lemon juice

1 tablespoon olive oil, plus extra for drizzling

a pinch of salt

about 300 ml warm water

pizza topping

1 recipe Pizza Maker's Tomato Sauce (page 228)

250 g fresh mozzarella cheese, thinly sliced

a good handful of fresh basil leaves

sea salt and freshly ground black pepper

2 pizza stones or baking sheets

2 baking sheets lined with non-stick baking parchment

serves 4

To make the dough, put the semolina flour in a bowl, crumble the fresh yeast into the flour, add the lemon juice, olive oil and a generous pinch of salt, then add enough warm water to form a very soft dough. Transfer to a floured work surface and knead for 10 minutes or until smooth and elastic. Put the dough in a clean, oiled bowl (or an oiled plastic bag), cover and let rise until doubled in size (about 1 hour).

Put the pizza stones or baking sheets in the oven and preheat the oven to 220°C (425°F) Gas 7.

Cut the dough in half and knead each half into a round. Pat or roll the rounds into 25 cm circles, keeping the bases well floured. Transfer the pizzas to baking sheets lined with non-stick baking parchment. Spread each one lightly with tomato sauce, cover with sliced mozzarella and season with salt and pepper. Let rise in a warm place for 10 minutes, then open the oven door and slide paper and pizza onto the hot pizza stones or baking sheets.

Bake in the preheated oven for 18–20 minutes, until the crust is golden and the cheese melted but still white. Remove from the oven, sprinkle with basil leaves and olive oil, then eat immediately.

Note Semolina flour is very finely ground and needs no extra flour. You can grind ordinary semolina into fine flour by working it in a blender for about 2 minutes.

roasted pepper pizza

Roasting peppers really brings out their sweetness. Make sure
the peppers are still warm when you add them to the dressing
so that they absorb the flavours of the garlic and parsley.

Put a pizza stone or baking sheet in the oven and preheat
the oven to 220°C (425°F) Gas 7. Put the peppers in a
small roasting tin and bake for 30 minutes, turning them
occasionally, until the skin blisters and blackens.

Meanwhile, put the garlic and parsley in a bowl. Add the oil
and salt and pepper to taste.

Remove the peppers from the oven, cover with a clean tea
towel and set aside for about 10 minutes until cool enough
to handle but still warm. Pierce the bottom of each pepper
and squeeze the juices into the parsley and oil mixture. Skin
and deseed the peppers. Cut the flesh into 2 cm strips and
add it to the mixture. Cover and leave at room temperature
until needed.

Roll out the pizza dough on a lightly floured work surface
to 30 cm diameter and brush with a little oil. Spoon over
the tomato sauce and arrange the sliced tomatoes and
mozzarella on top. Spoon the pepper mixture over the top.

Carefully transfer to the hot pizza stone or baking sheet and
cook in the preheated oven for 20–25 minutes until crisp
and golden. Serve immediately.

2 red peppers

2 yellow peppers

2 garlic cloves, finely chopped

a small bunch of flat leaf parsley,
finely chopped

2 tablespoons olive oil

1 recipe Basic Pizza Dough (page 231)

1 recipe Pizza Maker's Tomato Sauce
(page 228)

150 g tomatoes, sliced or halved

150 g mozzarella cheese, drained
and sliced

sea salt and freshly ground
black pepper

a pizza stone or baking sheet

serves **2**

Mushrooms are always an excellent choice for pizza toppings. For a range of flavours and textures, use a mixture of varieties, including chestnut, shiitake and field. The basil, chilli and garlic oil isn't essential, but adds a kick.

mushroom pizza *with basil, chilli and garlic oil*

1 recipe Basic Pizza Dough (page 231)

8 tablespoons olive oil

1 recipe Pizza Maker's Tomato Sauce (page 228)

400 g mixed mushrooms, thickly sliced

150 g mozzarella cheese, drained and chopped

2 plump garlic cloves, halved

1 large, mild red chilli, deseeded and quartered

8 fresh basil leaves, finely shredded

sea salt and freshly ground black pepper

a pizza stone or baking sheet

serves 2

Put a pizza stone or baking sheet in the oven and preheat the oven to 220°C (425°F) Gas 7.

Roll out the dough on a lightly floured work surface to 30 cm diameter and brush with a little oil. Spoon over the tomato sauce and top with the mushrooms and mozzarella.

Drizzle the pizza with a little oil and sprinkle with salt and pepper. Carefully transfer to the hot pizza stone or baking sheet and cook in the preheated oven for 20–25 minutes until crisp and golden.

Meanwhile, put the remaining oil in a small saucepan with the garlic and chilli. Heat very gently for 10 minutes until the garlic is softened and translucent. Remove the pan from the heat and let cool for 5 minutes.

Using a fork, remove and discard the garlic and chilli. Stir the basil into the oil, then drizzle it over the hot pizza. Serve immediately.

Bresaola, dried lean beef from the Alpine region of Italy, has a lovely sweetness which here complements the peppery rocket and salty Parmesan. If you can't find bresaola, use a dry-cure ham, such as prosciutto.

aubergine pizza *with bresaola, rocket and parmesan*

1 aubergine, cut into 1 cm slices

3–4 tablespoons olive oil, plus extra to serve

1 recipe Basic Pizza Dough (page 231)

1 recipe Pizza Maker's Tomato Sauce (page 228)

100 g very thinly sliced bresaola or cured ham

50 g rocket leaves

Parmesan cheese shavings

sea salt and freshly ground black pepper

a pizza stone or baking sheet

serves 2

Put a pizza stone or baking sheet in the oven and preheat the oven to 200°C (400°F) Gas 6.

Brush the aubergine slices with the oil and sprinkle salt and pepper lightly on both sides. Preheat a stove-top grill pan, add the aubergine slices and cook for 3–4 minutes on each side until tender and browned.

Roll out the dough on a lightly floured work surface to 30 cm diameter and brush with a little oil. Spoon over the tomato sauce and put the aubergine slices on top.

Transfer to the hot pizza stone or baking sheet and cook in the preheated oven for 15 minutes. Remove from the oven and ripple the bresaola or ham evenly across the pizza. Return the pizza to the oven and cook for a further 5–10 minutes until crisp and golden.

Sprinkle with the rocket leaves and Parmesan. Top with a splash of olive oil and a good grinding of black pepper. Serve immediately.

quattro stagioni pizza

The pizza for those who just can't make up their minds which one they want. You get all the best bits at once with this one.

4 tablespoons olive oil

1 shallot, thinly sliced

150 g chestnut mushrooms, sliced

2 tablespoons chopped fresh parsley

1 recipe Basic Pizza Dough (page 231)

1 recipe Pizza Maker's Tomato Sauce (page 228)

50 g Parma ham, shredded

6 black olives

4 artichoke hearts in oil, drained and quartered

75 g mozzarella cheese, drained and sliced

4 anchovy fillets in oil, drained

sea salt and freshly ground black pepper

fresh basil leaves, to serve

a pizza stone or baking sheet

serves 2

Put a pizza stone or baking sheet in the oven and preheat the oven to 200°C (400°F) Gas 6.

Heat 2 tablespoons of the oil in a frying pan, add the shallot and cook for 2 minutes. Add the mushrooms and cook for 2–3 minutes until softened and golden. Stir in the parsley and season with salt and pepper to taste.

Roll out the dough on a lightly floured work surface to 30 cm diameter and brush with a little oil. Spoon over the tomato sauce. Pile the mushrooms over one quarter of the pizza. Arrange the ham and olives on another quarter and the artichoke hearts on the third section of pizza. Lay the mozzarella on the remaining section and put the anchovies on top.

Drizzle a little more oil over the whole pizza and sprinkle with salt and plenty of black pepper. Carefully transfer to the hot pizza stone or baking sheet and cook in the preheated oven for 20–25 minutes until crisp and golden. Cut into quarters, sprinkle the basil over the artichoke portion and serve immediately.

In general, Italians like to stick to the classics when it comes to pizza, but as you can see below, pizza toppings are limitless. I have taken inspiration from a dish I had in Verona, and applied it to a pizza – well, it's just bread and cheese after all, isn't it?

potato pizza

15 g fresh yeast, 1 tablespoon dried active baking yeast, or 1 sachet easy-blend yeast

a pinch of sugar

250 ml warm water

350 g plain white flour, plus extra for dusting

1 tablespoon olive oil, plus extra for drizzling

a pinch of salt

potato topping

1 medium potato, peeled and sliced extremely thinly

150 g fontina, Taleggio or mozzarella cheese

1 large radicchio, cut into about 8 wedges, brushed with olive oil and grilled for 5 minutes

1 tablespoon chopped fresh thyme

sea salt and freshly ground black pepper

a baking tin, about 23 x 33 cm

serves 2–4

To make the dough, put the fresh yeast and sugar in a medium bowl and beat until creamy. Whisk in the warm water and leave for 10 minutes until frothy. For other yeasts, use according to the packet instructions.

Sift the flour into a large bowl and make a hollow in the centre. Pour in the yeast mixture, olive oil and a good pinch of salt. Mix with a round-bladed knife, then your hands, until the dough comes together. Transfer to a floured work surface, wash and dry your hands and knead for 10 minutes until smooth and elastic. The dough should be quite soft, but if too soft to handle, add more flour, 1 tablespoon at a time. Put the dough in a clean, oiled bowl, cover with a damp tea towel or clingfilm and let rise until doubled in size – about 1 hour.

When risen, punch down the dough with your fists, then roll out or pat into a rectangle that will fit in the baking tin, pushing it up the sides a little. Cover the top with a thin layer of sliced potato, then half the cheese. The wedges of radicchio, then the remaining cheese. Season with salt and pepper and sprinkle with thyme. Drizzle oil over the top and let rise in a warm place for 10 minutes.

Bake in a preheated oven at 220°C (425°F) Gas 7 for 15–20 minutes or until golden and bubbling. Serve immediately.

I will never forget this tart. I ate it right down in the toe of Italy on my way to Sicily. The tart was turned out before us on the little table – the tomatoes could not have been more red nor the basil more green and fresh.

tomato upside-down tart *with basil*

Cut the tomatoes in half around the middle. Arrange cut side up in the shallow tart tin, so that they fit tightly together. Mix the garlic and oregano with the olive oil, salt and pepper. Spoon or brush the mixture over the cut tomatoes.

Bake in a preheated oven at 160°C (325°F) Gas 3 for about 2 hours, checking from time to time. They should be slightly shrunk and still a brilliant red colour. If too dark, they will be bitter. Let cool in the tin (if the tin is very burned, wash it out, brush it with oil and return the tomatoes). Increase the oven temperature to 200°C (400°F) Gas 6.

Roll out the pastry on a lightly floured work surface to a circle slightly bigger than the tin. Using the rolling pin to help you, lift up the pastry and unroll it over the tin, letting the edges drape over the sides. Lightly press the pastry down over the tomatoes, but do not trim the edges yet. Bake for 20 minutes until golden.

Remove from the oven and let settle for 5 minutes, then trim off the overhanging edges and invert onto a plate. Sprinkle with olive oil and basil leaves and serve.

8–10 large ripe plum tomatoes (size depending on what will fit the tin)

2 garlic cloves, finely chopped

1 tablespoon dried oregano

4 tablespoons extra virgin olive oil, plus extra to serve

250 g puff pastry

sea salt and freshly ground black pepper

a good handful of fresh basil leaves, to serve

a shallow tart tin or sauté pan, 22 cm diameter

serves 4

Focaccia literally means 'a bread that was baked on the hearth', but it is easy to bake in conventional ovens. I make this one in a tin, but it can be shaped on a baking sheet to any shape you want. Although a rustic focaccia can be made with any basic pizza dough, the secret of a truly light focaccia lies in three risings, and dimpling the dough with your fingers so it traps olive oil while it bakes.

focaccia al rosmarino

750 g Italian '00' flour or plain white flour, plus extra for kneading

½ teaspoon fine salt

25 g fresh yeast (for dried yeast, follow the packet instructions)

150 ml good olive oil

450 ml warm water

coarse sea or crystal salt

sprigs of rosemary

a water spray

2 shallow cake tins, pie or pizza plates, 25 cm diameter, lightly oiled

makes 2 thick focacce, 25 cm diameter

Sift the flour and fine salt into a large bowl and make a hollow in the centre. Crumble in the yeast. Pour in 3 tablespoons of the olive oil, then rub in the yeast until the mixture resembles fine breadcrumbs. Pour in the warm water and mix with your hands until the dough comes together.

Transfer the dough to a floured work surface, wash and dry your hands and knead for 10 minutes until smooth and elastic. The dough should be quite soft, but if too soft to handle, knead in more flour, 1 tablespoon at a time. Put the dough in a clean, oiled bowl, cover with a damp tea towel or clingfilm and let rise in a warm place until doubled in size, 30–90 minutes.

Punch down the dough and cut it in half. Put on a floured work surface and shape each half into a round ball. Roll out into 2 circles, 25 cm diameter each, and put in the tins. Cover with a damp tea towel or clingfilm and let rise for 30 minutes.

Remove the tea towel and, using your fingertips, make dimples all over the surface of the dough. They can be quite deep. Pour over the remaining oil and sprinkle generously with coarse salt. Cover again and let rise for 30 minutes. Spray with water, sprinkle the rosemary on top and bake in a preheated oven at 200°C (400°F) Gas 6 for 20–25 minutes. Transfer to a wire rack to cool. Eat the same day or freeze immediately. Serve with a meal, or as a snack with oil and vinegar for dipping and olives.

rosemary and onion schiacciata

Schiacciata is the Tuscan word for flat bread, usually baked on the hearth. It is the ancestor of modern pizza.

To make the pizza dough, cream the fresh yeast with the sugar in a small bowl, then whisk in the warm water. Leave for 10 minutes until frothy. For other yeasts, follow the packet instructions.

Sift the flour into a large bowl and make a well in the centre. Pour in the yeast mixture, olive oil, salt and rosemary. Mix with a round-bladed knife, then bring the dough together with your hands. Tip out onto a floured work surface. With clean, dry hands, knead the dough for 10 minutes until smooth, elastic and quite soft. (If too soft to handle, knead in a little more flour.) Put in a clean oiled bowl, cover with a damp tea towel or cling film and let rise for about 1 hour or until doubled in size.

Finely slice the onions. Heat the oil in a heavy-based saucepan. Add the onions and cook over gentle heat, stirring occasionally, for 40 minutes to 1 hour until they are completely soft and golden – they must not brown. Stir in the chopped rosemary.

Punch down the dough with your hands and roll out, or stretch with your fingers, to a rectangle or 30 cm circle on the baking sheet. Spoon the onions on top of the pizza and spread them evenly. Dot with the mozzarella, anchovy fillets and olives. Sprinkle with olive oil.

Bake in a preheated oven at 230°C (450°F) Gas 8 for 15–20 minutes until golden and crisp. Top with rosemary leaves and serve immediately.

15 g fresh yeast, or 1 sachet easy-blend dried yeast

a pinch of sugar

250 ml warm water

350 g plain white flour

2 tablespoons olive oil

1/2 teaspoon salt

1 tablespoon chopped fresh rosemary

onion topping

1 kg onions

100 ml olive oil, plus extra for sprinkling

1 tablespoon chopped fresh rosemary

175 g mozzarella, thinly sliced

12 anchovy fillets in oil, drained

16 black olives, pitted

sprigs of rosemary

a large baking sheet, floured

makes a 30 cm pizza, serves 4

salads, vegetables and pulses

350 g waxy potatoes, peeled

175 g fine green beans, trimmed

extra virgin olive oil

50 g black or green olives, pitted

1 small crisp lettuce

2 large ripe tomatoes (or unripe to be authentic), peeled and quartered

3 tablespoons chopped fresh parsley

sea salt and freshly ground black pepper

to serve

a small bottle of good olive oil

a small bottle of red wine vinegar

serves 4

If you ask for a mixed salad in Italy, this is what you will get. Don't be surprised if the tomatoes are not red ripe, but hard and green – this is how they are eaten in salads. This dish is to cleanse the palate after a meat or fish course, and that is just what it does. Leaving the skins on potatoes and tomatoes is generally not done, but you can if you prefer.

italian mixed salad

Boil the potatoes in large saucepan of boiling salted water for about 15 minutes or until tender, adding the beans 4 minutes before the potatoes are ready. Drain and cover with cold water to stop them cooking further.

When cold, drain well. Transfer the beans to a bowl, slice the potatoes thickly and add to the beans, moistening with a little olive oil. Add the olives and toss well.

Wash the lettuce and tear it into bite-sized pieces. Add the lettuce and tomatoes to the potatoes and beans and toss lightly. Transfer to a serving bowl and sprinkle with parsley, salt and pepper. Serve the olive oil and vinegar separately and dress the salad at the table.

In Sicily, the land of orange and lemon groves, this salad is often served after grilled fish – especially in the region around Palermo. It is another example of their passion for sweet and savoury combinations and is very refreshing.

orange, endive and black olive salad

2 oranges

1 red onion

125 g escarole, curly endive or frisée

dressing

finely grated zest and juice of 1 unwaxed orange

6 tablespoons extra virgin olive oil

2 tablespoons thinly shredded fresh basil leaves

2 tablespoons finely chopped, pitted, Greek-style, oven dried black olives

2 sun-dried tomatoes in oil, finely chopped

sea salt and freshly ground black pepper

serves 4

To make the dressing, put the orange zest and juice, olive oil, basil, olives and sun-dried tomatoes in a large bowl. Mix well, season with salt and pepper and set aside to develop the flavours.

Peel the oranges with a sharp knife, removing all the skin and white pith. Divide into segments. Thinly slice the onion, using a very sharp thin-bladed knife or a Japanese mandolin. Immediately toss the onion and oranges in the dressing to prevent discoloration. Let marinate in a cool place for 15 minutes.

Put the escarole on a plate and pile the dressed orange and onion mixture on top, spooning over any remaining dressing. Serve immediately.

beetroot, wheat and rocket salad

Farro is an ancient form of wheat that is often used in Italy to make soups, salads and even puddings. You can find it in Italian delis, or under the name 'wheat berries' or 'wheat grain' in health food stores. It is delicious and chewy and makes a wonderful earthy salad combined with sweet beetroot and warm dressing. Barley makes a good substitute. The salad should be served warm.

Drain the soaked farro and put it in a large saucepan with the onion, carrot, celery, bay leaf and crushed garlic cloves. Add water to cover. Bring to the boil, turn down the heat and simmer for about 45 minutes or until tender and firm but not falling apart and mushy. Drain, then remove and discard the vegetables.

Heat 2 tablespoons of the olive oil in a frying pan and cook the pancetta until golden and crisp. Remove the pancetta, drain on kitchen paper and transfer to a large bowl. Return the pan to the heat and add the beetroot. Fry for 2–3 minutes, then add to the pancetta.

Add the chopped garlic to the hot pan and fry until just colouring. Immediately deglaze the pan with the red wine vinegar and add the sugar, boiling until it has dissolved. Pour in the remaining olive oil, stir well and heat gently but do not boil. Add salt and pepper to taste.

Add the farro, spring onions and rocket to the pancetta and beetroot in the bowl and mix gently. Pour in the dressing and toss lightly but thoroughly. Serve immediately before it becomes soggy.

300 g *farro* (or wheat grain), soaked in cold water for 2 hours

1 small onion, halved

1 carrot, peeled and halved

1 celery stalk, halved

1 bay leaf

2 whole garlic cloves, lightly crushed but kept whole

150 ml extra virgin olive oil

100 g pancetta cut into matchsticks

500 g small cooked beetroot, peeled and quartered

1 fat garlic clove, finely chopped

3 tablespoons red wine vinegar

1/2 teaspoon sugar

6 spring onions, white and green parts chopped

300 g rocket

sea salt and freshly ground black pepper

serves 4

In Sicily, onions are roasted in huge metal trays, then put on display outside vegetable shops. Sicilians love the sweetness of onions cooked like this. Normally the onions are simply squeezed out of their skins after roasting. However, I think they taste even better finished off with a sweet and sour sauce.

whole onions baked in their skins

Trim the root end of each onion so that they will stand up securely. Rub with olive oil. Cut a deep cross in the top of each one, slicing towards the base so that it is cut almost into quarters.

Pack closely together in a flameproof roasting tin. Sprinkle with olive oil, salt and pepper. Bake in a preheated oven at 190°C (375°F) Gas 5 for 1–1¼ hours until tender in the centre.

Transfer the onions to a serving dish, leaving the juices behind. Set the roasting tin over medium heat and add the wine, vinegar, sultanas, fennel seeds and capers. Scrape up any sediment and boil for a couple of minutes until reduced and syrupy.

Taste, add salt and pepper if necessary, then pour the sauce over the onions and sprinkle with chopped fresh parsley.

6 large white, red or purple onions

olive oil, for basting and serving

150 ml white wine

3 tablespoons red wine vinegar

2 tablespoons sultanas

1 teaspoon fennel seeds

1 tablespoon small salted capers, rinsed

sea salt and freshly ground black pepper

2–3 tablespoons chopped fresh flat leaf parsley, to serve

a flameproof roasting tin

serves 6

sicilian green vegetables

This is traditionally cooked for quite some time (about 45 minutes), because it used to be made with dried beans, but I have shortened the cooking time to keep the freshness and colour of the vegetables. It is often served as a soup, or you can add ricotta for a light lunch.

250 g shelled broad beans, fresh or frozen and thawed, (650 g before shelling)

4 tablespoons olive oil

250 g spring onions, coarsely chopped

4 baby fresh, canned or frozen artichoke hearts, quartered

300 ml Vegetable Stock (page 234) or water

250 g shelled peas, fresh or frozen and thawed (500 g before shelling)

a good pinch of sugar, to taste

2 tablespoons chopped fresh mint leaves

sea salt and freshly ground black pepper

serves 4

If using fresh artichokes, see the note on page 32 for how to prepare them. Drain them just before using.

Bring a large saucepan of salted water to the boil, add the broad beans and boil for 1 minute. Drain and plunge them into a bowl of cold water to cool them quickly and set the colour. Nick the skin at the top of a bean and gently squeeze at the bottom to pop it out. Continue until all are done.

Heat the oil in a heavy saucepan, add the spring onions and cook over gentle heat for a couple of minutes until they wilt and soften, but do not let them brown. Add the fresh artichokes, if using, then the stock or water. Season well with salt and pepper, bring to the boil, then reduce the heat and simmer for 5 minutes.

Add the peas and cook for 5 minutes, then gently stir in the beans and canned or preserved artichoke hearts, if using. Simmer for another 3–4 minutes. Remove the pan from the heat, taste, add a good pinch of sugar, then stir in the mint. Let cool so the flavours will develop. Serve at room temperature.

Fresh young artichokes are wonderful cooked in this simple way. They are easy to prepare, but it is worth wearing light rubber gloves to prevent black fingers. Baby artichokes are quite different from the fat, globe ones. They are slightly smaller than your hand, elongated, purple-green and usually sold in bunches.

pan-fried artichokes
with thyme and cool ricotta

8–12 baby purple-green artichokes with stems and heads, about 10 cm long, or 12 whole char-grilled deli artichokes in oil, drained

1½ lemons

100 ml good olive oil

1–2 tablespoons chopped fresh thyme

150 ml dry white wine

at least 125 g fresh ricotta cheese

sea salt and freshly ground black pepper

serves 4

If using fresh artichokes, see the note on page 32 for how to prepare them. When ready to cook them, drain and cut them in half lengthways.

Heat the oil in a large frying pan until hot, then add the artichokes. Fry for 3 minutes without moving them, then turn them over and cook for another 2–3 minutes until tender. If using store-bought char-grilled artichokes, cut them in half and reheat gently in the olive oil for 3–4 minutes. Transfer to a warm serving dish.

Add the thyme to the pan and cook over high heat for a few seconds to release the aroma. Add the wine and boil hard to reduce by half. Season with a squeeze of lemon juice, salt and pepper. Crumble the ricotta around the edge of the plate of artichokes and pour the hot thyme sauce on top. Serve immediately.

These firm but juicy tomatoes burst with the flavour of the sun. They take no time to prepare, but need a long time in the oven and smell fantastic while cooking. Plum tomatoes have less moisture and work well, but you can use any vine-ripened variety, just as long as they have some taste!

slow-roasted tomatoes
with garlic and oregano

6–10 ripe plum tomatoes

2 garlic cloves, finely chopped

1 tablespoon dried oregano

4 tablespoons extra virgin olive oil

sea salt and freshly ground black pepper

fresh basil leaves, to serve

a baking sheet covered with greaseproof paper

serves 4

Cut the tomatoes in half lengthways (around the middle if using round tomatoes). Put them cut side up on the baking sheet.

Put the garlic, oregano, olive oil, salt and pepper in a bowl and mix well, then spoon or brush the mixture over the cut tomatoes.

Bake in a preheated oven at 160°C (325°F) Gas 3 for 1½–2 hours, checking every now and then. The tomatoes should be slightly shrunk but still brilliantly red after cooking (If they are too dark, they will taste bitter).

Serve topped with fresh basil leaves as an accompaniment to grills and fish, or use on top of bruschetta.

These peppers are a vegetable and pasta course in one. They should be luscious and soft, with a wrinkled browned exterior. The garlicky cherry tomatoes keep the pasta moist, and the chilli and pecorino give a hint of sharpness. A delicious antipasto and also a good accompaniment for fish.

4 medium yellow or red peppers

50 g *capelli d'angelo* or very fine spaghetti

6 tablespoons extra virgin olive oil

12 ripe cherry tomatoes, quartered

2 garlic cloves, finely chopped

3 tablespoons chopped fresh basil leaves

50 g pine nuts, coarsely chopped

½ teaspoon dried chilli flakes (optional)

75 g freshly grated pecorino cheese

sea salt and freshly ground black pepper

a baking dish, lightly oiled

serves 4

roast peppers *stuffed with pasta and tomatoes*

Slice the tops off the peppers and reserve. Scrape out and discard all the seeds and white pith. Set the peppers upright in a lightly oiled dish small enough to fit them snugly. If they don't stand upright, shave a little piece off the base, but don't pierce right through.

Cook the pasta in plenty of boiling salted water according to the packet instructions, about 8 minutes. Drain well, then toss with 2 tablespoons of the olive oil.

Put the tomatoes in a bowl with another 2 tablespoons of oil, the garlic, basil, pine nuts, chilli flakes, if using, and pecorino and mix well. Season to taste with salt and pepper. Fill the peppers two-thirds full with the pasta, then spoon in the tomato mixture. Put the pepper lids on top and brush liberally all over with the remaining olive oil.

Bake in a preheated oven at 220°C (425°F) Gas 7 for 25–30 minutes or until the peppers start to wrinkle and blister. Serve hot or at room temperature.

My favourite recipe for sweet peppers is this one from Sicily. I never use green ones because I find them too bitter – they are just unripe red peppers and you need all that Mediterranean sunshine and sweetness trapped inside the red and yellow ones. When cooked, the peppers should be very soft and well caramelized for this recipe to be properly successful. Delicious on its own, this dish will also be great with a grilled steak.

sautéed peppers *with olives and capers*

Heat the oil in a large frying pan. Add the peppers and garlic cloves and cook over fairly high heat for 10 minutes, stirring often to prevent burning, until they start to caramelize. Alternatively, you can do this all in a roasting pan in a hot oven, roasting them at 220°C (425°F) Gas 7 for about 20 minutes, turning once. However, I would keep the garlic cloves whole in this case to prevent them from burning.

When well caramelized, stir in the anchovies and cook, stirring for about 2 minutes until they dissolve. Add the vinegar and stir-fry for a few minutes to let the flavours develop and the vinegar evaporate. Finally, stir in the capers and olives and continue to cook for a couple of minutes until heated through. Add salt and pepper to taste, then serve hot or at room temperature.

6 tablespoons extra virgin olive oil

2 medium red peppers, halved, deseeded and cut into thin strips

2 medium yellow peppers, halved, deseeded and cut into thin strips

4 garlic cloves, thinly sliced

6 anchovy fillets in oil, drained

3 tablespoons wine vinegar

2 tablespoons salted capers, rinsed and soaked in water for 10 minutes, then drained

125 g mixed whole black and green olives

sea salt and freshly ground black pepper

serves 4

Funghetto has nothing to do with mushrooms, as the name in Italian might suggest. It refers to a method of cooking involving a lot of hot oil. Frying cubed aubergines concentrates the flavour and creates a lovely brown crust on the sides, so don't shy away from it.

golden aubergines
with tomatoes and capers

2 medium aubergines, about 500 g

3 tablespoons salt

sunflower or olive oil, for cooking

2 tablespoons tomato purée or sun-dried tomato purée

1 tablespoon small capers in vinegar, drained

3 tablespoons chopped fresh flat leaf parley

2 garlic cloves, very finely chopped

sea salt and freshly ground black pepper

serves 4

Trim the aubergines and cut into bite-sized cubes, about 2 cm square. Half fill a large bowl with cold water and stir in the salt. Add the aubergines to the water and put a plate on top to hold them under the water. Set aside for 30 minutes, then remove the plate and drain through a colander. Rinse under cold water, then dry very well on a clean tea towel or with kitchen paper.

Pour 1 cm depth of oil into a wok or large frying pan. Heat until a piece of bread will sizzle instantly when it hits the oil. Cook the aubergines in batches until deep golden brown, about 5 minutes, then drain on kitchen paper.

Dilute the tomato purée with about 4 tablespoons water and add the capers. Pour into a large frying pan, bring to the boil, add the aubergines and toss well to coat with the tomato sauce. Add salt and pepper to taste. Mix the parsley and garlic together in a small bowl. Pile the aubergines in a warm dish, sprinkle with the parsley and garlic mixture and serve hot or warm.

My friend Louise, who lives in Italy, goes completely crazy for this dish. She always persuades me to put it on the menu for my guests on our cooking course in Tuscany, but it's really for her. It's very rich and deserves to be eaten on its own. It is said to originate in Campania and is often confused with *melanzane alla Parmigiana* – another dish altogether.

baked aubergine, tomato, mozzarella and parmesan

4 medium aubergines

2 tablespoons olive oil, plus extra for the aubergines

1 small onion, finely chopped

800 g canned chopped tomatoes, drained

2 tablespoons chopped fresh basil leaves

50–75 g freshly grated Parmesan cheese

200 g mozzarella cheese, thinly sliced

sea salt and freshly ground black pepper

a shallow oven dish, 25 cm diameter, lightly oiled

serves 4

Cut the aubergines lengthways into slices 1.25 cm wide. Soak them for 30 minutes in a bowl of heavily salted water.

Heat the oil in a frying pan, add the onion and cook for 5 minutes until softening, then add the tomatoes and basil and simmer gently for about 30 minutes. Season with salt and pepper.

Drain the aubergines, then rinse and pat dry with kitchen paper. Shallow fry them or brush with olive oil and roast in a preheated oven at 180°C (350°F) Gas 4 for about 20 minutes until deep golden brown. Set aside.

Arrange the aubergines in a single layer in the oven dish, then add a layer of grated Parmesan, followed by a layer of sliced mozzarella and a layer of the tomato sauce. Continue layering in this order until all the ingredients are used up, ending with a layer of sauce (this will keep the dish moist – if you want a crisp top, end with aubergine and Parmesan).

Bake in a preheated oven at 180°C (350°F) Gas 4 for 30–35 minutes until browned and bubbling. Remove from the oven and set aside for 10 minutes to settle before serving. Serve warm or at room temperature.

Courgettes are much more flavourful when cooked this way – bathed in garlic and olive oil, then stuffed with sweet, ripe cherry tomatoes and enveloped in melting fontina cheese. Delightfully fresh and summery.

courgettes and tomatoes *baked with fontina*

Cut the courgettes in half lengthways and trim a little off the uncut sides so that they will sit still like boats. Using a teaspoon, scoop out the soft-seeded centres, then arrange them in a row in the prepared dish.

Put the garlic, olive oil, salt and pepper in a bowl, stir well, then brush over the cut surfaces of the courgettes. Arrange the halved tomatoes in the grooves. Season well with salt and pepper then sprinkle with olive oil and breadcrumbs. Bake in a preheated oven at 180°C (350°F) Gas 4 for 30 minutes.

Remove from the oven and put the cheese slices on top of the courgettes and tomatoes. Return the dish to the oven for another 10–15 minutes to melt the cheese. Serve immediately while the cheese is still bubbling.

6 medium courgettes (as straight as possible)

2 garlic cloves, chopped

2 tablespoons olive oil, plus extra for sprinkling

about 30 cherry tomatoes, halved

3–4 tablespoons dried breadcrumbs

250 g fontina cheese, sliced

sea salt and freshly ground black pepper

a shallow ovenproof dish, greased

serves 6

The saltiness of pancetta or bacon is the perfect partner for courgettes, which are sweet, though they can be a little mild. The mixture of pancetta and thyme really brings out their flavour, as long as you cook it all over high heat to concentrate the juices and stop the courgettes becoming too wet.

courgettes sautéed
with pancetta and thyme

Trim the courgettes and cut them into cubes. Heat the oil in a frying pan, add the pancetta and fry until golden. Add the courgettes and fry over brisk heat for 3–4 minutes, tossing them around the pan from time to time until the cut sides start to turn golden.

When golden, add the thyme and plenty of black pepper (you probably won't need any salt). Season with a squeeze of lemon juice and serve immediately.

500 g courgettes

3 tablespoons olive oil

75 g pancetta cubes or lardons

1 tablespoon chopped fresh thyme

sea salt (optional) and freshly ground black pepper

freshly squeezed juice of ½ lemon

serves 4

fennel and leeks braised in cream and lemon

Fennel bulbs take on a completely different character when cooked slowly. They are soft and creamy with a very mild aniseed flavour more akin to celery. Sweet leeks balance it nicely, and the cream and lemon transform this into a very soothing dish. I like to serve this recipe with summery white fish dishes or chicken with a few extra fennel seeds and lemon zest toasted in olive oil sprinkled on top.

Trim the stalks, fronds and root ends from the fennel bulbs. Reserve any tender stalks and fronds and chop them to use for serving. Cut the bulbs into 4–6 wedges. Cook in boiling salted water for 10 minutes, then drain.

Trim the leeks, cut into thick rounds and rinse in cold water to remove any grit. Melt the butter in a shallow braising pan or deep frying pan with a lid. When foaming, add the leeks and fry over brisk heat for 1 minute. Add the fennel seeds, if using, then the lemon juice, lemon zest and wine. Bring to the boil and boil hard until reduced by half. Tuck in the fennel so it nestles into the leeks.

Put the cream, milk and grated nutmeg in a bowl, add salt and pepper to taste, stir well, then pour over the fennel and leeks. Slowly bring to the boil, then turn down the heat, cover and simmer very gently for about 35 minutes or until the fennel is tender at the thickest part. Serve immediately, sprinkled with any reserved chopped fennel fronds.

Note To cook in the oven, cover the dish with foil and bake for 35–40 minutes at 190°C (375°F) Gas 5.

2 medium fennel bulbs

2 large or 4 medium leeks (about 350 g after trimming)

50 g unsalted butter

1 teaspoon fennel seeds (optional)

finely grated zest and juice of 1 unwaxed lemon

2 tablespoons white wine or dry vermouth

200 ml double cream

200 ml milk

freshly grated nutmeg

sea salt and freshly ground black pepper

serves 4

Carrots are electric orange in Sicily and taste fantastic. Sicily is also the home of Marsala, which comes in all varieties from bone dry to rich and sweet, and I wish this selection were more widely available outside the home country. The nuttiness of the dry Marsala cooks into the sweet carrots, transforming them into something very special indeed.

carrots *with olive oil and marsala*

600 g carrots, peeled, or scraped if young

3 large garlic cloves, unpeeled

6 tablespoons extra virgin olive oil

300 ml dry Marsala (or 150 ml dry sherry mixed with 150 ml sweet Marsala)

sea salt and freshly ground black pepper

2 tablespoons chopped fresh flat leaf parsley, to serve

serves 6

Slice the carrots into thin rounds or sticks. Rinse well and pat dry. Crush the garlic cloves to open them up, but don't crush to a pulp. Heat the oil in a heavy frying pan until just warm, add the garlic and fry gently for 5 minutes until lightly golden. This will flavour the oil without too much harsh garlic taste. Remove and discard the garlic.

Add the carrots and cook over medium heat for 2–3 minutes, tossing them around occasionally. Pour in the Marsala, bring to the boil, then turn down to a simmer, cover and cook until the carrots are tender (about 10 minutes, depending on thickness). By this time, the Marsala will have emulsified with the olive oil to make a thin sauce – if there seems to be too much, lift out the carrots and boil the sauce hard to reduce it. Taste and season with salt and pepper. Transfer to a serving dish, top with the parsley and serve.

Someone once said that life is too short to stuff a mushroom: wrong! The light stuffing in this recipe complements the mushroom's rich meaty flavour. If using a cultivated type, add a shake of wild mushroom powder to the caps before you add the stuffing.

ricotta-stuffed mushrooms

6 large mushroom caps, such as portobello, flat open mushrooms or porcini, approximately 400 g

2 tablespoons olive oil, plus extra for brushing

2 garlic cloves, finely chopped

3 tablespoons chopped fresh flat leaf parsley

75 g black olives, pitted and chopped

6 mi-cuit (sun-blushed) tomatoes, sliced

a pinch of ground chilli flakes

250 g fresh ricotta cheese

sea salt and freshly ground black pepper

3 tablespoons freshly grated Parmesan or pecorino cheese, to serve

a baking sheet, oiled

serves 6

Pull the stalks off the mushrooms and chop the stalks finely. Heat the oil in a frying pan and add the chopped stalks, garlic, parsley and olives and fry for a couple of minutes to soften the garlic. Remove from the heat and transfer to a bowl. Stir in the tomatoes, chilli flakes, salt and pepper, then stir in the ricotta very briefly – it must not be smooth.

Brush the mushroom caps all over with olive oil and arrange them upon-side up on an oiled baking sheet. Spoon the filling into the mushrooms in loose mounds. Sprinkle with the grated cheese and bake in a preheated oven at 190°C (375°F) Gas 5 for 15–20 minutes or until the tops are pale golden. Serve immediately.

potato and mushroom gratin

1 kg medium potatoes

750 g flavoursome mushrooms such as dark flat cap, chestnut or portobello (or use fresh wild mushrooms)

extra virgin olive oil, for sprinkling

175 g stale (not dry) white breadcrumbs

4 tablespoons freshly grated Parmesan cheese

4 tablespoons chopped fresh flat leaf parsley

sea salt and freshly ground black pepper

a deep gratin or other ovenproof dish

serves 4

Baking sliced potatoes and mushrooms in layers allows the potatoes to absorb the juices and earthy flavour of the mushrooms. Use the darkest mushrooms you can find – they will have the best taste. You can mix fresh ones with reconstituted dried mushrooms for a more intense flavour, if you prefer.

Peel the potatoes and slice them thickly, putting them in a bowl of cold water as you go. Trim the mushrooms and slice thickly. Put half the potatoes in a layer in the bottom of the ovenproof dish, sprinkle with olive oil and cover with half the mushrooms.

Put the breadcrumbs, Parmesan, parsley, salt and pepper in a bowl and mix well. Spread half this mixture over the mushrooms, then sprinkle with more olive oil. Cover with a layer of the remaining potatoes, then a layer of the remaining mushrooms. Finally, sprinkle with the remaining breadcrumb mixture and more oil.

Cover with foil and bake in a preheated oven at 180°C (350°F) Gas 4 for 30 minutes. Uncover and cook for a further 30 minutes until the potatoes are tender and the top is golden brown.

Note If you blanch the potato slices first for 5 minutes in boiling salted water, they will take only 30 minutes to cook.

the devil's potatoes

500 g waxy yellow
potatoes, unpeeled

2 fresh red chillies

200 ml fruity olive oil

sea salt and freshly
ground black pepper

serves 4

A treat for potato and chilli lovers, this dish is simplicity
itself. It is important to use a good olive oil because it is
very much a part of the dish. I use the large new potatoes
from Cyprus which have an almost creamy texture and
absorb the olive oil well. However, you can use any
potatoes – it will work with almost anything.

Boil the potatoes whole in a large saucepan of salted water.

While they are boiling, cut the chillies in half lengthways, remove the
seeds and chop the flesh finely (wear rubber gloves to protect your
fingers if you like). Heat the olive oil very gently in a small frying pan
and add the chillies – they should delicately fizzle when added. Stir
briefly, then remove from the heat. Add salt and pepper to taste.

When the potatoes are cooked, drain well. When they are cool enough
to handle, slice thickly and arrange half the slices in a single layer in
a serving dish. Pour half the chilli oil over the potatoes, then add the
remaining potatoes and pour over the remaining oil. Cover with kitchen
foil and let stand for 10 minutes before serving with a little extra salt
and pepper. They should be served warm.

Any type of dried bean will work here – only the cooking times will differ. To make sure that the onion isn't too strong, soak the slices in cold water for 10 minutes. Alternatively, you could blanch them for 1 minute in boiling water, to which a squeeze of lemon juice has been added.

cannellini beans *with olive oil and mint*

Soak the beans overnight in three times their volume of cold water. The next day, drain and put them in a large saucepan. Add the garlic cloves, the whole mint leaves and pepper. Cover with cold water, slowly bring to the boil, then turn down the heat and simmer for 25–30 minutes until tender. Times will vary according to the freshness of the beans. Drain well and remove the garlic and mint.

Put the olive oil, chopped mint and onion in a bowl and mix with a fork. Add the drained beans to the bowl and toss them carefully in the dressing. Taste and check the seasoning – you may have to add salt. Serve warm or at room temperature.

400 g dried cannellini, haricot or navy beans

2 garlic cloves, unpeeled but smashed open

6–8 whole mint leaves, plus 3 tablespoons chopped or torn mint leaves

6 tablespoons extra virgin olive oil

1 small red onion, thinly sliced into rings or half moons

sea salt and freshly ground black pepper

serves 4

A rich, wintry stew of lentils, onions and herbs – perfect to serve with game dishes, duck and of course, meaty Italian sausages. Sometimes, it is even better served on its own with a stack of char-grilled bread, rubbed with garlic and sprinkled with olive oil, as a filling supper dish in front of a crackling log fire. Red wine is the only accompaniment.

lentils braised *with little onions and herbs*

12 small pickling onions

2 tablespoons olive oil

50 g pancetta cubes or lardons

2 carrots, finely chopped

2 celery stalks, finely chopped

3 garlic cloves, finely chopped

3 bay leaves

a sprig of rosemary

2–3 sprigs of thyme

350 g brown lentils

100 ml light dry red wine

1 tablespoon balsamic vinegar

3 tablespoons chopped fresh flat leaf parsley

25 g unsalted butter

sea salt and freshly ground black pepper

serves 6

To peel the onions, put them in a bowl and cover with boiling water. Leave for 2–3 minutes, then drain. Peel off the loosened skins while they are still warm, leaving the onions whole. Trim the root end, but not completely, because this will hold them together.

Heat the oil in a saucepan or casserole and add the pancetta cubes. Cook slowly for 5 minutes to release the fat, then add the carrots, celery and garlic. Stir well and cook over medium heat for about 5 minutes until beginning to soften. Add the bay leaves, rosemary, thyme, onions, lentils, wine and vinegar. Cook over high heat for 1 minute, then add enough water to cover everything completely. Season to taste with salt and pepper. Bring to the boil, turn down the heat, cover and simmer gently for about 40 minutes until the lentils are completely soft and they have absorbed most of the liquid.

Remove the pan from the heat and remove and discard the herbs. Stir in the chopped parsley and the butter, then serve immediately.

fish

500 g small squid, cleaned

8 raw prawns (optional)

1 kg fresh mussels and clams*

1.75 kg mixed whole but cleaned fish (see note on fish choice)

flavoured broth

150 ml extra virgin olive oil

4 medium leeks, sliced and well washed

4 garlic cloves, finely chopped

300 ml dry white wine

a large pinch of saffron threads

750 g ripe red plum tomatoes, coarsely chopped

30 ml sun-dried tomato paste or purée or 6 sun-dried tomatoes in oil, drained and coarsely chopped

1 teaspoon fennel seeds

1 tablespoon dried oregano

sea salt and freshly ground black pepper

to serve

lemon wedges

handfuls of chopped fresh flat leaf parsley

crusty bread

serves 6–8

*Scrub and debeard the mussels. Tap any open mussels and clams against the work surface. Discard any that don't close – they are dead – and also any with damaged shells. Keep in a bowl of cold water until ready to cook.

This stew is the perfect family feast. A well-flavoured base broth is essential, including saffron and fennel seeds, and the fish is then poached in this stock. The fish is served separately and the broth is ladled on top.

a big fish stew

To make the broth, heat the olive oil in a large, deep, heavy casserole pot and add the leeks and garlic. Cook gently for about 5 minutes until softened. Pour in the white wine and boil rapidly until reduced by half. Add the saffron, tomatoes, tomato paste, fennel seeds and oregano. Pour in 600 ml water and bring to the boil. Turn down the heat, cover and simmer for 20 minutes until the tomatoes and oil separate.

Start cooking the fish. Add the squid to the pan and poach for 3–4 minutes. Remove with a slotted spoon, put on a plate, cover and keep them warm. Add the prawns, if using, and simmer just until opaque. Remove with a slotted spoon and keep warm with the squid. Add the mussels and clams to the broth, cover and boil for a few minutes until they open. Remove with a slotted spoon and keep them warm. Discard any that haven't opened.

Poach all the remaining fish in the broth until just cooked. Remove from the broth, arrange on a serving dish and set the mussels, squid and prawns on top. Taste the broth, which will have all the flavours of the cooked fish in it, and add salt and pepper if necessary. Moisten the fish with some broth and serve the rest separately with the lemon wedges, parsley and lots of crusty bread.

Fish choice Choose at least 4 varieties – the greater the variety, the more intense the flavour. Do not choose oily fish like salmon, herring or sardines. Choose from: slipper lobster (*cigales de mer*), conger eel, shark, red gurnard, cod, hake, John Dory, red mullet, monkfish, swordfish, rascasse, weaver, whiting or wrasse.

fish baked in a salt crust

This excellent method of cooking fish conserves the juices without in any way oversalting the flesh. The salt bakes hard to form a protective crust so that the fish cooks in its own juices – the skin protects it from the salt. It's a nice idea to stuff the cavity with fresh herbs and sliced lemon before burying the fish in salt.

at least 1 kg fine sea salt

1 egg white

1–2 kg whole large firm-fleshed fish, gutted but not scaled

a tomato salad, to serve

a long ovenproof dish (choose one that will comfortably hold the whole fish)

serves 4–6

Pour enough salt into the dish to make a layer 2.5 cm thick. Mix the egg white with 3 tablespoons water and sprinkle half the liquid over the salt. Set the fish on the salt bed and pour enough salt around and over it to cover it completely. Sprinkle with the remaining egg white and water.

Bake the fish in a preheated oven at 190°C (375°F) Gas 5 for 45 minutes to 1 hour.

Remove from the oven and put the dish, with the fish still encased in its snowy armour, in the middle of the table. Crack open the salt crust with a rolling pin. Remove the shards of salt crust and peel back the skin to reveal perfectly cooked, succulent flesh without a trace of saltiness.

Serve with a simple tomato salad.

When opened up and boned, sardines cook in minutes in a hot oven. Marinating them in oil and lemon juice lends piquancy to the delicate flesh. This is a good dish to prepare a day ahead, then serve for lunch with salad.

sardines baked *with garlic, lemon, olive oil and breadcrumbs*

Scale the sardines with the blunt edge of a knife. Cut off the heads and slit open the bellies. Remove the guts under running water. Slide your thumb along the backbone to release the flesh along its length. Take hold of the backbone at the head end and lift it out. The fish should now be open flat like a book.

Put the oil, lemon zest and juice in a large bowl, whisk well, then stir in the garlic, parsley, capers, salt and pepper. Holding each sardine by the tail, dip in the lemony olive oil, then put skin side up in the ovenproof dish. Pour in any remaining liquid, sprinkle with the breadcrumbs and bake in a preheated oven at 200°C (400°F) Gas 6 for 15 minutes.

Serve warm immediately or let cool and store overnight in the refrigerator. Serve the next day at room temperature, when the sardines will have marinated in the oil, lemon and herbs. Add the parsley and lemon wedges, then serve.

8 fresh whole sardines

100 ml good olive oil

finely grated zest and juice of 1 unwaxed lemon

2 garlic cloves, thinly sliced

3 tablespoons chopped fresh flat leaf parsley, plus extra to serve

1 tablespoon salted capers, rinsed, drained and chopped

3 tablespoons dried breadcrumbs

sea salt and freshly ground black pepper

lemon wedges, to serve

a shallow ovenproof dish

serves 4

Sea bass has a wonderful, clean, fresh taste and cooking in parchment is the best way to cook whole fish (with the possible exception of grilling over embers). The parchment lets the fish steam in its own juices, absorbing the aroma of the fresh herbs and lemon. This cooking time should be perfect – the fish is better slightly underdone at the bone than overdone. Open the wrapped fish at the table so you can appreciate the full aroma.

sea bass baked in parchment

Cut 2 large rectangles of baking parchment big enough to wrap each fish generously. Brush the rectangles with a little oil.

Season the cavities of the fish with salt and pepper. Put 2 bay leaves in each one and tuck in the thyme and lemon slices.

Put one fish on one half of the paper, sprinkle with white wine or lemon juice, fold over the other half loosely and twist or fold the edges tightly together to seal. Repeat with the other fish, then put both packets on the baking tray.

Bake in a preheated oven at 190°C (375°F) Gas 5 for 20 minutes. Serve immediately, opening the packets at the table.

2 sea bass, about 350 g each, cleaned and scaled

about 1 tablespoon olive oil

4 fresh bay leaves

2 sprigs of thyme

6 thin slices of lemon

about 2 tablespoons dry white wine or freshly squeezed lemon juice

sea salt and freshly ground black pepper

a baking tray

serves 2

This dish originated in Venice during the Renaissance and has been cooked and served on gondolas on the eve of the Feast of the Redeemer in July ever since. As well as adding flavour to the delicate fish, the marinade slightly preserves it too. This dish can also be made with sardines, but sole is popular in Venice.

fillets of sole *in sweet and sour onion marinade*

8 sole fillets, skinned

plain flour, for dusting

100 ml olive oil

sea salt and freshly ground black pepper

sweet and sour marinade

50 ml olive oil

2 mild onions, thinly sliced

3 bay leaves or a sprig

100 ml white wine vinegar

to serve

salad

crusty bread

serves 4

To make the marinade, heat the olive oil in a frying pan over medium heat. Add the onions and bay leaves. Cook, stirring, for 15–20 minutes. The onions should be softened and translucent and not browned at all. Add the vinegar and boil rapidly for a few minutes until amalgamated with the onion juices. Remove from the heat, pour into a bowl and set aside.

Season the sole fillets with salt, and dip them in flour to coat both sides, shaking to remove the excess. Heat the olive oil in a frying pan and fry the sole fillets for about 1 minute on each side. Remove the sole and drain on kitchen paper.

Spoon half of the cooked and cooled marinade into a shallow dish, season with pepper and arrange the sole fillets on top. Pour in the remaining marinade, cover with clingfilm and let marinate for several hours or overnight in the refrigerator.

Serve at room temperature with a salad and some crusty bread.

Fresh tuna bakes very well in the oven, especially if
marinated first to keep it moist. I have taken the
liberty of adding capers and mint to the traditional
salmoriglio sauce adored by Sicilians. The capers add
a sharp edge to the sauce and cut through the
richness of the fish.

oven-baked tuna *with salsa*

3 tablespoons good olive oil

4 garlic cloves, crushed

1 teaspoon dried oregano

4 tablespoons dry white wine

1 lemon, thinly sliced

4 thick tuna steaks

sea salt and freshly ground
black pepper

caper and mint salsa

1 tablespoon salted capers

2 tablespoons red wine vinegar

1–2 teaspoons sugar

finely grated zest and juice of
½ unwaxed lemon

4 tablespoons good olive oil

1 garlic clove, finely chopped

2 tablespoons finely chopped
fresh mint leaves

a non-aluminium ovenproof dish

serves 4

Put the olive oil, garlic, oregano, wine, salt and pepper in a bowl
and stir well. Spread half the lemon slices in the ovenproof dish
and put the tuna steaks on top. Pour over the olive oil mixture and
put the remaining lemon slices on top. Set aside for 30 minutes.

Meanwhile, to make the salsa, soak the capers in water for
10 minutes, then drain, pat dry and chop if large. Put the vinegar
and sugar in a bowl and stir until the sugar has dissolved. Add the
lemon zest and juice. Whisk in the olive oil, then add the garlic,
chopped mint and capers. Set aside to infuse.

Bake the tuna in a preheated oven at 180°C (350°F) Gas 4 for
about 12 minutes. The fish should be just cooked in the centre –
it can be served slightly pink. Lift onto warm plates, leaving the
juices behind. Serve with the salsa spooned over the top.

Tuna is a very rich meat and is always cut thinly in Italy – never as thick as the seared steaks we are used to. Marinating the slices in mustard and grappa gives them a piquant crust – so good with the sweet peppers.

grilled tuna steaks *with peperonata*

To make the marinade, crush the garlic, put it in a bowl and beat in the mustard and grappa. Season with salt and pepper and use to spread over the cut sides of the tuna. Arrange in a non-metal dish, cover and let marinate in a cool place for about 1 hour.

To make the peperonata, heat 3 tablespoons of the oil in a saucepan, then add the tomatoes and chilli flakes. Cook over medium heat for about 10 minutes until the tomatoes disintegrate.

Heat the remaining oil in a frying pan, add the onions, garlic and peppers and sauté for about 10 minutes until softening. Add the pepper mixture to the tomatoes and simmer, covered, for 45 minutes until very soft. Taste and season with salt and pepper.

Preheat the grill or barbecue. Sprinkle the steaks with olive oil and arrange on a rack over a foil-lined grill pan. Grill for about 2 minutes on each side until crusty on the outside and still pink in the middle. Alternatively, barbecue over hot embers for slightly less time. Serve with the peperonata, which can be served hot or cold.

4 tuna loin steaks cut 1.25 cm thick

olive oil, for grilling

sea salt and freshly ground black pepper

marinade

4 garlic cloves

3 tablespoons Dijon mustard

2 tablespoons grappa or brandy

peperonata

6 tablespoons olive oil

1 kg fresh ripe tomatoes, skinned, deseeded and chopped, or 800 g canned chopped tomatoes

$^1/_2$ teaspoon dried chilli flakes

2 medium onions, thinly sliced

3 garlic cloves, chopped

3 large red peppers, halved, deseeded and cut into thin strips

serves 4

meat and poultry

chicken roasted *with bay leaves, lemon and garlic*

A memorable way of roasting a chicken – all the flavours permeate the flesh during its time in the oven, and the smell in the kitchen is wonderful. This dish is particularly good eaten cold at a picnic.

Starting at the vent end of the chicken, slide your hand carefully underneath the skin of each breast to loosen it. Push 3–4 slices of lemon under the skin of each breast, slide the garlic slices on top of the lemon, then finish with 3 bay leaves on each side. Smooth down the skin. Rub with olive oil, then with salt and pepper.

Arrange a bed of bay leaves in the roasting tin and put the remaining lemon slices on top. Put the chicken on top and roast in a preheated oven at 190°C (375°F) Gas 5 for 20 minutes per 500 g, plus 20 minutes extra, basting every now and then, until golden brown, crisp and cooked through. To check, push a skewer into the thickest part of the thigh – the juices should run clear and golden. If there is any trace of pink, cook for a further 5–10 minutes and check again.

Serve hot, or cool, chill and serve cold.

1 free-range chicken, about 1.5 kg

1 lemon, very thinly sliced

3 garlic cloves, thinly sliced

6 small fresh bay leaves (or use sage or even basil), plus extra to make a bed

a little olive oil

sea salt and freshly ground black pepper

a roasting tin

serves 6

A magnificent way to cook lamb long and slowly, especially if it is not as young as it might be. Liver is often served with onions cooked to melting sweetness, and this is a similar technique. The black olives enrich the dish and give it a smoky taste. The cutlets can be finished off in a medium hot oven instead of cooking on top. They are good reheated.

braised lamb cutlets
with onions, herbs and olives

Season the meat on both sides with salt and pepper.

Heat half the oil in a large sauté pan until very hot, then add the cutlets and quickly brown on both sides. Remove to a plate and let cool.

Heat the remaining oil in the same pan and add the onions. Cook over gentle heat for 15 minutes, stirring occasionally, until the onions begin to soften – do not let them brown. Stir in the herbs, anchovies, olives, salt and pepper.

Arrange the cutlets on top of the bed of onions in the pan and cover with a lid. Cook over very low heat for 20 minutes, watching that the onions don't catch and burn. Serve topped with rosemary sprigs.

8–12 lamb cutlets, depending on size

100 ml olive oil

900 g onions, thinly sliced

2 tablespoons chopped fresh oregano and rosemary, mixed

4 anchovy fillets in oil, drained, rinsed and chopped

15 black olives, pitted

sea salt and freshly ground black pepper

rosemary sprigs, to serve

serves 4

leg of lamb

This leg of lamb is braised until cooked and tender, then roasted to colour it. The powerful flavourings melt into the meat, with the anchovies disappearing to leave a salty note. This way of cooking lamb stems from the Roman Empire, when the most popular condiment was a sauce made from fermented fish.

1.5 kg leg of lamb

2 tablespoons olive oil

10 juniper berries

3 garlic cloves, crushed

55 g salted anchovies, boned and rinsed, or canned anchovies

1 tablespoon chopped fresh rosemary

2 tablespoons balsamic vinegar

2 sprigs of rosemary

2 fresh bay leaves

300 ml dry white wine

sprigs of fresh thyme

sea salt and freshly ground black pepper

a flameproof casserole dish (into which the lamb should fit snugly)

serves 6

Trim the lamb of any excess fat. Heat the oil in the casserole dish, add the lamb and brown it all over. Remove and let cool.

Crush 6 of the juniper berries, the garlic, anchovies and chopped rosemary with a mortar and pestle. Stir in the vinegar and mix to a paste. Using a small, sharp knife, make lots of small incisions in the lamb. Spread the juniper paste all over the meat, working it into the incisions, then season with salt and pepper.

Put the rosemary sprigs and bay leaves in the casserole dish and set the lamb on top. Pour in the wine. Crush the remaining juniper berries and add to the lamb, then add the thyme. Cover the casserole, bring to the boil on top of the stove, then braise in a preheated oven at 160°C (325°F) Gas 3 for 1 hour, turning the lamb every 20 minutes.

Raise the oven temperature to 200°C (400°F) Gas 6. Roast uncovered for another 45 minutes or until browned – the lamb should be very tender and cooked through.

Transfer the lamb to a serving dish and keep it warm. Skim off the fat from the pan, then boil the sauce, adding a little water if necessary and scraping up the sediment. Season with salt and pepper if necessary and serve with the lamb.

pork loin roasted
with rosemary and garlic

This is a classic oven-baked Tuscan dish. Redolent of the early morning markets where *porchetta* is sold crammed into huge buns, this dish recreates all those tastes and smells in your oven at home. Use plenty of rosemary in this dish.

Turn the loin fat side down. Make deep slits all over, especially in the thick part. Put the garlic, rosemary and at least 1 teaspoon of salt and pepper (more will give a truly authentic Tuscan flavour) into a food processor and blend to a paste. Push this paste into all the slits in the meat and spread the remainder over the surface of the meat. Roll up and tie with fine string.

Weigh the meat and calculate the cooking time, allowing 25 minutes for every 500 g. At this stage you can cover with clingfilm and chill for several hours to deepen the flavour. When ready to cook, preheat the oven to 230°C (450°F) Gas 8, or as high as your oven will go. Uncover the pork and brown all over in a hot frying pan. Transfer the pork to a roasting tin, pour over the wine and tuck in the rosemary sprigs.

Put the bones in the other roasting tin, convex side up. Rub the skin with a little oil and salt, then drape it over the bones. Put the tin on the top shelf of the oven, and the pork loin on the bottom or middle shelf. Roast for 20 minutes. Turn down the heat to 200°C (400°F) Gas 6, and roast for the remaining calculated time, basting the pork loin every 20 minutes.

Remove the pork from the oven and let rest in a warm place for 15 minutes before carving into thick slices. Serve with shards of crunchy crackling and the pan juices.

1.75 kg loin of pork on the bone*

6 large garlic cloves

4 tablespoons chopped fresh rosemary

300 ml dry white wine

sprigs of fresh rosemary

olive oil, for brushing

sea salt and freshly ground black pepper

2 roasting tins

serves 6

Ask the butcher to bone the loin (but to give you the bones) and to remove the skin and score it for the crackling

beefsteak *with rocket*

Italians love meat cooked very rare: you will often see a slip of a girl tucking into a steak that would comfortably feed two – and she will eat it all. The steaks are produced from the huge, handsome, white Chianina cattle, native to Tuscany.

Brush the steaks with olive oil and season very well with salt and pepper. Heat a stove-top grill pan or light a barbecue. When the pan is smoking hot, add the steaks and cook for 2 minutes on each side to seal, then lower the heat and continue to cook for about 4 minutes on each side for medium-rare steaks, less for rare.

Transfer the steaks to a cutting board and slice them thickly. Put a pile of rocket on 4 warm plates and arrange the sliced meat on top. Pour any juices from the steaks onto the meat and serve immediately, sprinkled with chopped parsley.

4 sirloin steaks, about 200 g each

2 tablespoons olive oil

200 g wild rocket (*rucola*)

sea salt and freshly ground black pepper

chopped fresh parsley, to serve

serves 4

2 bottles Barolo or other good-quality red wine, 750 ml each

1.5 kg stewing beef such as shin, chuck or skirt, well trimmed

2 onions, coarsely chopped

2 carrots, chopped

1 celery stalk, chopped

2 bay leaves

2 large sprigs of thyme

6 peppercorns

2 allspice berries, crushed

3 tablespoons olive oil

2 tablespoons tomato purée or sun-dried tomato purée

about 1.5 litres beef stock, to cover

sea salt and freshly ground black pepper

chopped fresh flat leaf parsley, to serve

a large flameproof casserole dish

serves 6–8

Cut the meat into very large chunks – long, slow cooking tenderizes it perfectly. Served with boiled potatoes and green vegetables, this is a good dish for a crowd.

beef braised in red wine

Pour the wine into a large saucepan and bring to the boil. Boil hard until reduced by half (leaving 750 ml). Let cool completely.

Cut the meat into 5 cm pieces. Put in a large plastic bag with the onions, carrots, celery, bay leaves, thyme, peppercorns and allspice. Pour in the cooled wine. Shake the bag to mix, then seal the bag and put it in a large bowl to marinate in the refrigerator overnight.

Open the bag and pour the contents into a colander set over a bowl. Separate the meat from the vegetable mixture and pat the meat pieces dry with kitchen paper. Reserve the wine.

Heat the oil in the casserole dish on top of the stove and brown the meat well in batches. Return the meat to the dish, then stir in the vegetable mixture. Add the reserved wine and stir in the tomato purée. Add enough stock to cover the meat and vegetables. Bring to the boil, reduce the heat, cover, and cook in a preheated oven at 160°C (325°F) Gas 3 for 2–3 hours until very tender. Top up the liquid with extra stock if it evaporates too quickly. Alternatively, the dish may be simmered gently on top of the stove for 2–3 hours.

Using a slotted spoon, transfer the meat to a bowl. Discard the bay leaves. Pour the sauce into a blender or food processor and blend until smooth (the sauce will look pale, but will darken when reheated). Add salt and pepper to taste. The sauce should be quite thick – if not, boil to reduce it. Stir the meat back into the sauce, reheat, sprinkle with parsley, and serve.

The Tuscans have a reputation for being great game hunters. In the past, when they used to cook little gamebirds, or *uccelletti*, they would generally season them with sage. This dish contains no *uccelletti*, but it is cooked in the same way – the sausages take the place of the birds. This is the most famous way to cook beans and is equally delicious served with roast pork.

grilled sausages
with tomato and sage bean stew

500 g dried cannellini or haricot beans or, if lucky, 1 kg fresh cannellini or borlotti beans

a pinch of bicarbonate of soda

8 fat fresh Italian pork sausages, or all-meat pork sausages

90 ml olive oil

3 garlic cloves, crushed

about 10 fresh sage leaves

350 g fresh ripe tomatoes, skinned, deseeded and puréed, or 300 ml tomato passata (strained, crushed tomatoes)

sea salt and freshly ground black pepper

serves 4

If using dried beans, cover with plenty of cold water and soak overnight. The next day, drain and rinse them, then cook in plenty of boiling water without any salt, but with a pinch of bicarbonate of soda (to keep the skins soft) for 1–1½ hours, or until tender. Drain. If using fresh beans, shell and boil them in slightly salted water until ready, 25–30 minutes, then drain.

Brush the sausages with oil and grill or barbecue for 15 minutes until tender and crisp on the outside.

Meanwhile, heat the oil in a saucepan and add the garlic, sage and black pepper. Fry until the garlic is golden and the sage beginning to become transparent and crisp. Remove and reserve a few crisp leaves for serving.

Add the puréed tomatoes to the pan, heat to simmering, then add the cooked beans. Cook for 10 minutes, then taste and adjust the seasoning with salt and pepper. Serve the sausages with the beans and top with the reserved crisp sage leaves.

sweet things

It's worth making a journey to Italy just to taste lemons that have been properly ripened in the sun. Walk through a lemon grove when the glossy green trees are in blossom and the scent is intoxicating. The beautiful leaves can be used like bay leaves or the more exotic Thai lime leaves to impart a lemony flavour to sweet and savoury dishes alike. I mix the orange with the lemon juice because it softens the acidity of our un-sunkissed lemons.

sorbetto al limone

300 g caster sugar

finely grated zest and juice of 6 unwaxed lemons, plus 6 medium, even-sized lemons

finely grated zest and juice of 1 unwaxed orange

an ice cream maker

serves 6

Put the sugar and 600 ml water in a saucepan with the lemon and orange zest. Bring slowly to the boil and boil rapidly for 3–4 minutes. Remove the pan from the heat and let cool. Meanwhile, strain the fruit juices into a bowl. When the syrup is cold, strain into the bowl of juice. Chill. When cold, churn it in an ice cream maker according to the manufacturer's instructions.

Meanwhile, cut the tops off the remaining 6 lemons and shave a little off each base so that it will stand up. Scoop out the insides, squeeze and keep the juice for another time. Put the shells in the freezer. When the sorbet is frozen, fill the lemon shells with it and set the tops back on. Return to the freezer until needed. Soften in the refrigerator for 10–15 minutes before serving.

mint sorbet

Italians are very fond of sweet and sticky liqueurs, so I have laced this sorbetto with crème de menthe – bliss.

250 g caster sugar

200 ml dry white wine, such as sauvignon blanc, chilled

60 g fresh mint leaves

2 tablespoons fresh lime juice

2–3 tablespoons crème de menthe liqueur

an ice cream maker

makes about 1 litre

Put the sugar and 450 ml water in a saucepan and bring slowly to the boil, stirring until the sugar dissolves. Remove from the heat, then stir in the wine and 40 g of the mint leaves. Let cool, then chill for several hours. Strain the syrup into a blender. Add the remaining mint leaves, lime juice and liqueur. Blend until the leaves disappear and the syrup is speckled green.

Pour into an ice cream maker and freeze according to the manufacturer's instructions. Transfer to a chilled freezer container, cover and freeze until firm. Let soften in the refrigerator for 20 minutes before serving.

cantaloupe melon ice cream

1 small, very ripe orange-fleshed cantaloupe or charentais melon, about 1.25 kg, halved and deseeded

150 g caster sugar

3 tablespoons golden syrup

1 tablespoon freshly squeezed lemon juice

750 ml full-cream milk

60 g skimmed milk powder

1 teaspoon powdered gelatine

an ice cream maker

serves 8

Use the ripest, most fragrant, orange-fleshed melon for this. Add a dash of melon liqueur if lacking in flavour.

Scoop out the melon flesh into a food processor or blender. Add the sugar, syrup and lemon juice and purée until smooth.

Pour the milk into a saucepan and whisk in the dried milk powder and gelatine. Bring slowly to just below the boil. Stir in the melon purée and transfer to a bowl to cool. When cold, chill in the refrigerator for at least 1 hour or overnight.

When thoroughly chilled, transfer to an ice cream maker and freeze according to the manufacturer's instructions. Transfer to a chilled freezer container, cover and freeze until firm. Let soften in the refrigerator for 20 minutes before serving.

watermelon sorbetto
with chocolate chip seeds

A beautiful pink, exotic *sorbetto* from Sicily, delicately perfumed with a hint of cinnamon. Just for fun, chocolate chips have been added to represent the black watermelon seeds, but they do give the sorbet a nice crunchy texture.

Remove the seeds from the melon with the tip of a small knife. Put the flesh in a food processor and purée until smooth. With the machine running, pour in the sugar and blend for 30 seconds.

Pour the melon mixture into a saucepan and add the cinnamon stick. Slowly bring to the boil, stirring all the time to dissolve the sugar completely, then turn down the heat to a bare simmer for 1 minute. Remove from the heat, add the lemon juice and a few drops of pink food colouring if necessary. Let cool. When cold, remove the cinnamon stick and chill the mixture in the refrigerator for at least 1 hour (or overnight – this makes freezing quicker).

Transfer to an ice cream maker and freeze according to the manufacturer's instructions. Stir in the chocolate chips when the sorbetto is still soft. Transfer to a chilled freezer container, cover and freeze until firm. Let soften in the refrigerator for 20 minutes before serving.

Alternatively, pour the cooled melon mixture in a shallow freezer tray and freeze until the sorbetto is frozen around the edges. Mash well with a fork. When it is half frozen again, blend in a food processor until creamy, stir in the chocolate chips, then cover and freeze until firm. Let soften in the refrigerator for 20 minutes before serving.

750 g red watermelon flesh, cut into cubes

150 g caster sugar (or a bit less if the melon is very sweet)

1 small cinnamon stick

freshly squeezed juice of 2 ripe lemons

a little pink food colouring, if necessary

75 g plain chocolate chips

an ice cream maker*

serves 4–6

*Freeze in an ice cream maker for the best results

There is nothing quite as sensual as warm zabaglione served straight from the pan. Many like to beat it in a copper bowl so that it cooks quickly. The secret is not to let the mixture get too hot, but still hot enough to cook and thicken the egg yolks. It must be made at the last moment, but it doesn't take long and is well worth the effort.

zabaglione

2 large egg yolks

2 tablespoons sweet Marsala wine

2 tablespoons caster sugar

savoiardi or sponge fingers, for dipping

serves 2

Put the egg yolks, Marsala and sugar in a medium heatproof bowl (preferably copper or stainless steel) and beat with a hand-held electric mixer or a whisk until well blended.

Set the bowl over a saucepan of gently simmering water – the bottom should at no time be in contact with the water. Do not let the water boil. Whisk the mixture until it is glossy, pale, light and fluffy and holds a trail when dropped from the whisk. This should take about 5 minutes. Serve immediately in warmed cocktail glasses with sponge fingers for dipping.

Variation To make chilled zabaglione for two, when cooked, remove the bowl from the heat and whisk until completely cold. In a separate bowl, whisk 150 ml double cream until floppy, then fold into the cold zabaglione. Spoon into glasses and chill the mixture for 2–3 hours before serving.

This is one of the best ways of cooking pears. It is so simple to make, but tastes luxurious. Choose pears that are ripe but not too soft, or they will overcook in the oven. If you can't get a good rich Marsala or Vin Santo, use sweet sherry or Madeira instead.

caramelized pears *with marsala and mascarpone cream*

6 large ripe pears

150 g caster sugar

150 ml Marsala or Vin Santo

200 g mascarpone cheese

1 vanilla pod, split, seeds scraped out and reserved

a flameproof, ovenproof pan or dish

serves 6

Cut the pears in half and scoop out the cores – do not peel them. Sprinkle the sugar into the flameproof pan or dish, set it over medium heat and let the sugar melt and caramelize. Remove from the heat as soon as it reaches a medium-brown colour and quickly arrange the pears cut side down in the caramel.

Bake in a preheated oven at 190°C (375°F) Gas 5 until the pears are soft, 20–25 minutes. Carefully lift out the pears and transfer to an ovenproof serving dish, keeping the caramel in the pan.

Put the pan on top of the stove over medium heat and add the Marsala or Vin Santo. Bring to the boil, stirring to dislodge any set caramel, and boil fast until reduced and syrupy. Set aside.

Scoop out a good teaspoon from each cooked pear and put it in a bowl. Add the mascarpone and vanilla seeds and beat well. Fill the centres of the pears with the mascarpone mixture. Return to the oven for 5 minutes until it has heated through. Serve with the caramel sauce spooned over the top.

Ripe figs need almost nothing done to them – but if you bake them with lots of vanilla- and lemon-scented sugar, and hide a walnut in the middle of each one, you will end up with something divine! Take care not to overcook them or they will collapse.

figs baked *with vanilla and lemon*

12 large ripe figs

12 walnut halves

2 soft, plump
vanilla pods

125 g sugar

grated zest of
1 unwaxed lemon

3 tablespoons
white wine

thick double cream or
ice cream, to serve

a shallow ovenproof dish

serves 6

Cut a deep cross in the top of each fig so that they open up a little. Push a walnut half into each cross. Pack the figs closely together in the baking dish.

Chop the vanilla pods and put them in a food processor. Add the sugar and lemon zest and process until the pods and lemon zest are chopped into tiny bits. Spoon some mixture over each fig and around the dish. Moisten with the white wine.

Bake in a preheated oven at 230°C (450°F) Gas 8 for 10 minutes until the sugar melts and the figs start to caramelize. Remove from the oven and let cool for a few minutes before serving with thick cream. Alternatively, serve cold with ice cream.

A refreshing change from the French *tarte au citron*. The almonds give the tart more body and add another flavour dimension. Traditionally, freshly ground almonds are used, because they have a fine, creamy texture and a better flavour than the ready-ground kind.

lemon and almond tart

To make the *pasta frolla*, work the butter into the flour and sugar until it looks like grated Parmesan cheese.

Put the 2 egg yolks in a small bowl, add 1 tablespoon water and beat lightly. Add to the flour mixture and knead lightly until smooth. Knead into a ball, flatten, then wrap in clingfilm and let it rest for 30 minutes.

Roll out the pastry on a floured work surface and use to line the tart tin. Prick the base all over with a fork, then chill or freeze for 15 minutes to set the pastry. Line with foil, flicking the edges inwards towards the centre so that it doesn't catch on the pastry. Fill with baking beans, set on the baking sheet and bake blind in the centre of a preheated oven at 190°C (375°F) Gas 5 for 10–12 minutes.

Remove the foil and beans and return the pastry case to the oven for a further 5–7 minutes to dry out completely.

To make the filling, put the eggs, sugar, lemon zest and juice in a bowl and whisk until light and fluffy. Stir in the melted butter and almonds. Mix well and pour into the prepared pastry case. Bake for 25–30 minutes, until the crust and the top of the tart is golden brown. Let cool, then chill before serving with whipped cream.

pasta frolla (shortcrust pastry)

200 g butter

300 g plain flour

100 g caster sugar

2 egg yolks

lemon and almond filling

4 large eggs, lightly beaten

120 g caster sugar

finely grated zest and juice of 3 unwaxed lemons

120 g unsalted butter, melted

120 g ground almonds

whipped cream, to serve

a fluted tart tin, 22 cm diameter

foil and baking beans

a baking sheet

serves 8

This amazingly popular pudding is said to have originated in Venice in the 1950s, and is one pudding that actually benefits from being made the day before. For added texture, grind real chocolate in a blender for layering and sprinkling.

tiramisù *with raspberries*

150 g plain dark chocolate, with over 60 per cent cocoa solids

250 g mascarpone cheese

5 tablespoons caster sugar

6 tablespoons Marsala wine

2 tablespoons dark rum

2 egg yolks

300 ml double cream, whipped to form soft peaks

100 ml Italian espresso coffee

24 savoiardi or sponge fingers

200 g fresh raspberries, plus extra to serve

a serving dish or 4 glasses

serves 4 generously

Put the chocolate in a blender or food processor and grind to a powder. Set aside. Put the mascarpone in a bowl and whisk in 3 tablespoons sugar, then beat in 2 tablespoons Marsala and the rum. Set aside.

To make the zabaglione mixture, put the egg yolks, 2 tablespoons Marsala and the remaining 2 tablespoons sugar in a medium heatproof bowl and beat with a hand-held electric mixer or whisk until blended. Set the bowl over a saucepan of gently simmering water – the bottom of the bowl should at no time be in contact with the water, and don't let the water boil. Whisk the mixture until it is glossy, pale, light and fluffy and holds a trail when dropped from the whisk, about 5 minutes. Remove the bowl from the heat and whisk until cold. Fold in the whipped cream, then fold in the mascarpone mixture.

Pour the espresso into a bowl and stir in 2 tablespoons Marsala. Dip the savoiardi, one at a time, into the espresso. Do not leave them in for too long or they will disintegrate. Arrange half the dipped savoiardi in the bottom of a serving dish or 4 glasses. Trickle over some more espresso, then add a layer of raspberries.

Sprinkle with one-third of the ground chocolate, then spoon over half the zabaglione-cream-mascarpone mixture. Arrange the remaining dipped savoiardi on top, moisten with any remaining espresso, add some more raspberries and sprinkle with half the remaining chocolate. Finally spoon over the remaining zabaglione-cream-mascarpone mixture and finish with a thick layer of chocolate and a few extra raspberries. Chill in the refrigerator for at least 3 hours (overnight is better) for the flavours to develop. Serve chilled.

amaretti biscuits *with pine nuts*

Delicious, crisp little biscuits made with a mixture of freshly ground almonds and pine nuts. If you have any peach or apricot kernels, use these in place of some of the almonds and they will impart a fantastic almond flavour – in this case, don't add the almond essence. These are wonderful used as the base for a trifle or eaten with after-dinner liqueurs.

100 g blanched almonds

?/??? ?? pine nuts, plus 3 tablespoons *extra*, for sprinkling

90 g caster sugar

2 large egg whites

1 teaspoon almond essence

a piping bag fitted with a plain 1.25 cm nozzle

2 baking sheets, lined with baking parchment

a wire rack

makes about 30

Put the almonds, pine nuts and 1 tablespoon of the caster sugar in a food processor fitted with the grater disc. Grind to a fine powder. Alternatively, use a blender or rotary nut grinder. Set aside.

Put the egg whites in a bowl and beat with a hand-held electric mixer until stiff but not dry. Gradually whisk in the remaining sugar until the whites are stiff and shiny. Fold in the ground nuts and almond essence. Spoon the mixture into the piping bag and pipe the mixture onto the baking sheets in tiny rounds.

Sprinkle with a few extra pine nuts and bake in a preheated oven at 150°C (300°F) Gas 2 for 30 minutes until the biscuits are lightly browned and hard. Transfer to a wire rack to cool. The biscuits may be stored in an airtight container for up to 2 weeks.

These biscuits are deliciously buttery and crunchy, and fantastic dipped into Vin Santo or *caffelatte*. These *biscotti* are cooked once in a log, then sliced and cooked again to dry them out. I like to add polenta for a slightly gritty texture.

hazelnut and chocolate biscotti

Spread the hazelnuts on a baking sheet and toast in a preheated oven at 160°C (325°F) Gas 3 for 5–10 minutes until they begin to release their aromas. Transfer the hazelnuts to a clean tea towel and rub off the skins. Let cool.

Put the butter and sugar in a bowl and beat until pale and creamy. Beat in the eggs, vanilla extract and rum. Using a separate bowl, sift together the flour, cocoa, baking powder and salt, then stir in the polenta. Fold into the butter and egg mixture. Stir in the toasted hazelnuts.

Transfer the dough to a floured work surface and knead until smooth. The dough should be soft but not sticky – if it feels sticky, add a little more flour. Divide the dough into 4 pieces. Roll into logs about 5 cm wide and 1.5 cm high. Flatten them slightly, then put on the prepared baking sheets. Bake for 35 minutes or until just golden around the edges.

Let cool slightly then, using a serrated knife, cut diagonally into 1 cm thick slices. Arrange cut side down on the baking sheets and bake for another 10–15 minutes until golden brown and crisp. (Take care not to let them burn, or they will taste bitter.) Transfer to a wire rack to cool. Store in an airtight container for up to 1 week.

200 g whole hazelnuts

125 g unsalted butter, softened

200 g sugar

2 eggs, beaten

2 teaspoons vanilla extract

1 tablespoon dark rum

300 g plain flour

75 g cocoa powder

1 1/2 teaspoons baking powder

1/2 teaspoon salt

75 g coarse polenta

2 baking sheets, lined with baking parchment

a wire rack

makes about 30

I have always loved the name of these little chocolate and almond biscuits from Piedmont in northern Italy. They are delicious and often made for special occasions such as christening teas and weddings.

lady's kisses

125 g ground almonds

a pinch of salt

125 g unsalted butter, at room temperature

125 g caster sugar

1 teaspoon vanilla extract

100 g plain flour

2 tablespoons cocoa powder

chocolate cream

100 g plain chocolate (over 60 per cent cocoa solids)

75 ml double cream

2 baking sheets, lined with non-stick baking parchment

a wire rack

makes about 24

Put the ground almonds and salt in a bowl and mix well. Put the butter, sugar and vanilla in another bowl and beat until pale and fluffy. Fold in the ground almonds, sift the flour and cocoa powder over the top and fold in.

Scoop out teaspoons of mixture and roll into small balls. Arrange the balls spaced well apart on the baking sheets. Press each one to flatten slightly.

Bake in a preheated oven at 180°C (350°F) Gas 4 for 15 minutes or until firm. Transfer onto wire racks to cool.

To make the chocolate cream, put the chocolate and cream in a bowl set over a saucepan of simmering water and heat gently until melted. When melted, remove the bowl from the pan and let cool to room temperature. Beat with a hand-held electric mixer until cold and thick, then chill until firm.

Bring the chocolate cream to room temperature, then use it to sandwich together 2 biscuits at a time. Pile on a plate and serve.

This dark, moist chocolate cake is made all over southern Italy, but particularly in Capri. Normally, it is made using ground almonds, but I have adapted this one to suit those who prefer not to eat nuts – it is equally delicious with a fantastic soft texture. Serve with whipped cream.

dark chocolate cake

flour, for dusting

250 g plain chocolate
(over 60 per cent cocoa solids)

250 g unsalted butter, softened

4 tablespoons espresso coffee

6 eggs, separated

200 g caster sugar

50 g potato flour or cornflour

1/2 teaspoon baking powder

150 g stale white breadcrumbs

icing sugar, for dusting

whipped cream, to serve

a springform cake tin, 25 cm diameter, sides well buttered, base-lined with non-stick baking parchment

a wire rack

makes one 25 cm cake

Dust the prepared cake tin with flour.

Break up the chocolate and put it in a heatproof bowl. Add the butter. Set over a saucepan of simmering water and stir occasionally until melted. Remove from the heat, stir in the coffee, then let cool a little.

Put the egg yolks and half the sugar in a bowl and beat until pale and fluffy. Mix in the potato flour and baking powder. Carefully mix in the chocolate and butter mixture, then fold in the breadcrumbs.

Put the egg whites in a bowl, whisk until stiff but not dry, then gradually whisk in the remaining sugar. Gently fold into the mixture. Pour into the prepared cake tin and bake in a preheated oven at 180°C (350°F) Gas 4 for about 30 minutes, until risen and almost firm in the centre. To test, insert a skewer into the middle of the cake. When removed it should have a little of the mixture clinging to it – this will ensure that the cake is moist. Do not overbake. Invert onto a wire rack to cool, then dust with icing sugar. Serve with whipped cream.

Note To make a smaller cake, halve the quantities and bake in a 20 cm cake tin.

Fluffy little puffs like this are very popular, and are found in many guises. There is usually one to suit each saint, for his or her particular Saint's Day. Deep-fried snacks like these are part of Italian life and are seen as a real festive treat.

fluffy ricotta fritters

250 g ricotta cheese

2 eggs, at room temperature

2 tablespoons sugar

1 teaspoon vanilla extract

120 g plain flour

1 teaspoon baking powder

½ teaspoon salt

vegetable oil, for deep-frying

icing sugar, to serve

an electric deep-fryer

a tray lined with kitchen paper

serves 4–6

Push the ricotta through a food mill, potato ricer or sieve into a large bowl. Put the eggs, sugar and vanilla in another bowl and whisk until pale and light. Fold into the ricotta.

Sift the flour with the baking powder and salt into a bowl, then fold it into the cheese and egg mixture.

Heat the vegetable oil in the deep-fryer to 190°C (375°F). Have a tray lined with kitchen paper and a slotted spoon or strainer at the ready.

Drop level tablespoons of the mixture into the hot oil in batches of 6. Fry for 2–3 minutes until puffed and deep brown all over (you may have to turn them in the oil). Drain and serve immediately, dusted with icing sugar.

basics

classic pesto

2 garlic cloves

55 g pine nuts

55 g fresh basil leaves
without stalks

150 ml good olive oil, plus extra
for sealing

55 g unsalted butter, softened

4 tablespoons freshly grated
Parmesan or aged
pecorino cheese

sea salt and freshly ground
black pepper

serves 4

When made with the freshest of ingredients, this sauce from Liguria is a brilliant green. It can turn a simple bowl of pasta or a piece of cold chicken into a dish that will transport you back to heady summer days.

Classic method Using a mortar and pestle, pound the garlic with a little salt and the pine nuts until broken up. Add the basil leaves, a few at a time, pounding and mixing to a paste. Gradually beat in the olive oil, little by little, until the mixture is creamy and thick. Beat in the butter and season with pepper, then beat in the cheese. Spoon into a jar with a layer of olive oil on top to exclude the air. Store in the refrigerator until needed, making sure you level the surface each time you use it, and re-cover with olive oil.

For those without much time or a mortar and pestle Put everything in a blender or food processor and process until the pesto is as smooth as you like it to be.

1 large red pepper

55 g fresh basil leaves
without stalks

1 garlic clove, crushed

2 tablespoons pine nuts, toasted

2 very ripe tomatoes

6 sun-dried tomatoes in oil,
drained

3 tablespoons tomato purée

$\frac{1}{2}$ teaspoon mild chilli powder

55 g freshly grated Parmesan or
aged pecorino cheese

150 ml extra virgin olive oil

serves 4

red pesto

Long before red pesto appeared in jars, I made this punchy, robust sauce to remind me of southern Italy. The chilli is essential, giving a special kick.

Grill the whole pepper, turning until blackened all over. Peel off the skin under running water, halve the pepper and remove the stalk and seeds.

Put the flesh in a food processor with the basil, garlic, pine nuts, tomatoes, sun-dried tomatoes, tomato purée, chilli powder and cheese and blend until smooth. With the machine running, slowly pour in the olive oil. Spoon into a jar and cover with a layer of olive oil. This will keep in the refrigerator for up to 2 weeks, topped up with olive oil as you use it.

pizza maker's tomato sauce

Pizzaiola sauce is named after the traditional sauce that a pizza maker would put on the base of a pizza. It is a speciality of Naples, but common throughout Italy. This sauce has a hundred different uses and is particularly delicious served with steaks and grilled or barbecued fish.

Put the oil in a large shallow pan and heat almost to smoking point (a wok is good for this). Standing back (it will splutter if it's at the right temperature), add the garlic, oregano and tomatoes.

Cook over a fierce heat for 5–8 minutes or until the sauce is thick and glossy. Season with salt and pepper.

8 tablespoons olive oil

2 garlic cloves, chopped

1 teaspoon dried (not fresh) oregano

800 g fresh tomatoes, skinned and coarsely chopped, or 800 g canned chopped tomatoes

sea salt and freshly ground black pepper

serves 4

béchamel sauce

This creamy sauce is the basis of many comforting pasta dishes, and equally good with meat, vegetable and fish dishes. The secret is to use more butter than flour and cook the flour in the butter for at least 5 minutes before adding the milk. To prevent lumps, I take the pan off the heat and add the cold milk all at once, whisking furiously before returning it to the heat to thicken and cook.

Melt the butter in a medium saucepan. When foaming, add the flour and cook over gentle heat for about 5 minutes without letting it brown. Have a balloon whisk ready. Slide off the heat and add all the milk at once, whisking very well. When all the flour and butter have been amalgamated and there are no lumps, return to the heat and slowly bring to the boil, whisking all the time. When it comes to the boil, add salt, simmer gently for 2–3 minutes, then use immediately.

If making in advance, cover the surface directly with clingfilm to prevent a skin forming, then let cool. When reheating, remove the clingfilm and reheat very gently, stirring every now and then until liquid. (You may need to whisk it to remove lumps.) If using for lasagne, don't worry too much about lumps – they will disappear when the whole dish cooks. If you like a thinner sauce, just add extra milk after it has boiled and thickened.

75 g butter

55 g plain white flour

about 500 ml milk

sea salt

makes 500 ml

basic pizza dough

250 g Italian '00' flour or strong white bread flour, plus extra for sprinkling

½ teaspoon salt

7 g sachet easy-blend dried yeast

2 tablespoons olive oil

125 ml warm water

serves 4

For a really good pizza dough, try to use the superfine durum wheat '00' flour, which you can buy in Italian stores and large supermarkets. Otherwise, choose a strong white bread flour. You can add flavourings such as chopped herbs or grated cheese to the dough, but you may prefer to let the toppings take centre stage.

Put the flour, salt and yeast in a large bowl and mix. Make a well in the centre. Add the oil and water to the well and gradually work in the flour to make a soft dough. Sprinkle over a little flour if the mixture feels too sticky, but make sure it is not too dry: the dough should be pliable and smooth.

Transfer the dough to a lightly floured work surface. Knead for 10 minutes, sprinkling with flour when needed, until the dough is smooth and stretchy.

Rub garlic oil over the surface of the dough and return the dough to the bowl. Cover with a clean tea towel and leave for about 1 hour, until the dough has doubled in size.

Remove the dough to a lightly floured work surface and knead for 2 minutes, until the excess air is knocked out. Roll out the dough according to the recipe you are following.

Nothing beats homemade pasta – not even shop-bought 'fresh'.
The texture is silky and the cooked dough itself very light.

fresh egg pasta

200 g plain flour
(or use 100 g Italian
'00' flour and 100 g
farina di semola)

a pinch of salt

2 medium eggs

1 tablespoon olive oil,
plus extra for coating

*a pasta machine or
rolling pin*

serves 2–4

Sift the flour and salt onto a clean work surface and make a
hollow in the centre with your fist. Put the eggs and olive oil in a
bowl, beat well, then pour into the hollow in the flour. Gradually
mix the eggs into the flour with the fingers of one hand, and bring
it together to form a dough.

Knead the pasta until smooth, lightly massage with a hint of olive
oil, put in a plastic bag and let rest for at least 30 minutes before
rolling out. The pasta will be much more elastic after resting. Roll
out by hand or by machine.

If using a machine, feed the rested dough several times through
the widest setting first, folding in 3 each time. Then roll the pasta
through all the settings, reducing the settings until reaching the
required thickness. Generally, the second from last setting is best
for tagliatelle, the finest being for ravioli or pasta that is to be filled.

After the required thickness is reached, hang the pasta over a
broom handle to dry a little – this will make cutting it easier in
humid weather, because it will not be so sticky.

Pass the pasta through the chosen cutters then drape the cut
pasta over the broom handle again until ready to cook.

Variation Spinach Pasta *Pasta Verde*

Cook 150 g frozen spinach according to the packet instructions,
drain, then squeeze out as much moisture as possible. As for the
main recipe, above, sift the flour onto a clean work surface and
make a hollow in the middle. Put the spinach, 1 large egg (instead
of 2 medium), salt and pepper in a blender and blend until
smooth. Pour this mixture into the hollow in the flour and proceed
as in the main recipe.

Too many vegetable stocks are insipid or taste of a single ingredient. This stock is extravagant in its use of vegetables, but will have very good flavour. Stock gives body and depth of flavour to dishes such as risotto, but shouldn't dominate the dish. Strong root vegetables such as turnips and parsnips are not good additions, and neither are potatoes or cabbage. Remember to wash everything first or you will end up with gritty stock.

vegetable stock

1 large onion, quartered

2 large carrots, quartered

1 small bunch of celery, coarsely chopped (including leaves)

2 leeks, white parts only, halved lengthways, rinsed and halved again

4 courgettes, thickly sliced

2 tomatoes, halved around the middle and seeds squeezed out

1 fennel bulb, quartered

1 Cos lettuce heart, coarsely chopped

3 garlic cloves

1 dried red chilli

4 fresh bay leaves

a handful of parsley stalks, crushed

1/2 lemon, sliced

6 black peppercorns

sea salt

makes 2–3 litres

Put all the ingredients in a large stockpot. Add water to cover, about 4 litres, and bring to the boil. As soon as it boils, reduce the heat and simmer for 15 minutes. Stir the stock and skim off the foam, then cook at the barest simmer for 1 hour, skimming often.

Remove the pot from the heat and strain the stock into a bowl through a colander lined with muslin. Discard the contents of the colander after they have cooled. Let the stock cool, then refrigerate it for several hours.

At this stage you can reboil the stock to concentrate it, or cover and chill in the refrigerator or freeze until needed. The stock will keep in the refrigerator for 3 days or the freezer for up to 6 months.

index

A

almonds: amaretti biscuits 215
  lady's kisses 219
  lemon and almond tart 211
amaretti biscuits with pine nuts 215
anchovies: leg of lamb 186
  marinated fresh anchovies 20
  mozzarella in carrozza 39
  pasta with puttanesca sauce 82
  quattro stagioni pizza 112–13
  rosemary and onion *schiacciata* 120
  spinach with pine nuts and 12
  white spaghetti 81
antipasti and snacks 8–39
artichokes: artichoke, pesto and pine nut
  bruschetta 32
  pan-fried artichokes with thyme and
  cool ricotta 135
  quattro stagioni pizza 112–13
asparagus with egg and truffle butter 11
aubergines: aubergine pizza with
  bresaola, rocket and Parmesan 111
  baked aubergine, tomato, mozzarella
  and Parmesan 145
  golden aubergines with tomatoes
  and capers 142
  pan-grilled aubergines with lemon,
  mint and balsamic vinegar 19
  spaghetti with aubergine and tomato
  sauce 74
  sweet and sour Sicilian aubergine
  stew 16

B

bacon: pasta with carbonara sauce 89
  see also pancetta
basil: classic pesto 226
  red pesto 226
  tomato sauce with double basil 80
beans *see* cannellini beans
béchamel sauce 229

beef: beef braised in red wine 193
  beefsteak with rocket 190
  lasagne al forno 90
beetroot, wheat and rocket salad 128
biscuits: amaretti biscuits 215
  hazelnut and chocolate biscotti 216
  lady's kisses 219
bread: creamy tomato and bread
  soup 42
  focaccia al rosmarino 119
  mozzarella in carrozza 39
  rosemary and onion *schiacciata* 120
  see also bruschetta
bresaola, aubergine pizza with 111
broad beans: Sicilian green
  vegetables 132
bruschetta: artichoke, pesto and pine
  nut 32
  grilled fig and prosciutto with rocket 36
  olive oil and garlic 31
  spicy garlic prawns on 35
  traditional peasant tomato and
  garlic 28

C

cabbage: *la ribollita* 45
cake, dark chocolate 220
cannellini beans: cannellini beans with
  olive oil and mint 160
  grilled sausages with tomato and sage
  bean stew 194
  pasta and bean soup 50
  la ribollita 45
cannelloni with ricotta, bitter greens and
  cherry tomato sauce 78
cantaloupe melon ice cream 200
caponata 16
caramelized pears 207
carbonara sauce, pasta with 89
carrots with olive oil and Marsala 152
cheese: aubergine pizza with bresaola,
  rocket and Parmesan 111
  baked aubergine, tomato, mozzarella
  and Parmesan 145

baked polenta with fontina and
  pancetta 93
courgettes and tomatoes baked with
  fontina 147
creamy radicchio and mascarpone
  risotto 63
creamy tomato and bread soup 42
fluffy ricotta fritters 223
Margherita pizza 104
mozzarella and sun-blushed tomato
  risotto 56
mozzarella in carrozza 39
mushroom mezzalune 77
mushroom pizza with basil, chilli and
  garlic oil 108
pan-fried artichokes with thyme and
  cool ricotta 135
Parma ham with figs and balsamic
  dressing 23
Parmesan and butter risotto 55
polenta baked with Italian sausage and
  cheese 97
potato pizza 115
quattro stagioni pizza 112–13
red wine risotto 64
ricotta-stuffed mushrooms 155
roasted pepper pizza 107
Roman gnocchi with herbs and
  semolina 98
rosemary and onion *schiacciata* 120
spinach broth with egg and cheese 46
sweet and sour Sicilian aubergine
  stew 16
chicken: chicken and mushroom
  risotto 68
  chicken roasted with bay leaves, lemon
  and garlic 182
chicken livers: lasagne al forno 90
chickpea flour: Sicilian chickpea and
  rosemary fritters 27
chickpeas, spicy garlic prawns with
  tomatoes and 35
chillies: the devil's potatoes 159
  mushroom pizza with basil, chilli and
  garlic oil 108

pasta with puttanesca sauce 82
chocolate: dark chocolate cake 220
  hazelnut and chocolate biscotti 216
  lady's kisses 219
  tiramisù with raspberries 212
  watermelon sorbetto with chocolate chip seeds 203
coffee: tiramisù with raspberries 212
courgettes: courgette and mint fritters 15
  courgettes and tomatoes baked with fontina 147
  courgettes sautéed with pancetta and thyme 149

D
the devil's potatoes 159
dough, basic pizza 231

E
eggs: asparagus with egg and truffle butter 11
  fresh egg pasta 232
  pasta with carbonara sauce 89
  spinach broth with egg and cheese 46
  zabaglione 204
endive, orange and black olive salad 127

F
fennel and leeks braised in cream and lemon 150
figs: figs baked with vanilla and lemon 208
  grilled fig and prosciutto bruschetta 36
  Parma ham with figs and balsamic dressing 23
fish 164–79
  big fish stew 167
  fish baked in a salt crust 168
  see also individual types of fish
focaccia al rosmarino 119
fritters: courgette and mint 15
  deep-fried sage leaves 24
  fluffy ricotta 223
  Sicilian chickpea and rosemary 27

G
gnocchi with herbs and semolina 98
gratin, potato and mushroom 156

H
ham: ham and leek risotto 71
  Parma ham with figs and balsamic dressing 23
  see also Parma ham
hazelnut and chocolate biscotti 216

I
ice cream, cantaloupe melon 200
Italian mixed salad 124

L
lady's kisses 219
lamb: braised lamb cutlets 185
  leg of lamb 186
lasagne al forno 90
leeks: big fish stew 167
  fennel and leeks braised in cream and lemon 150
  ham and leek risotto 71
lemon: lemon and almond tart 211
  marinated fresh anchovies 20
  sorbetto al limone 199
lentils braised with little onions and herbs 163

M
Margherita pizza 104
Marsala see wine
mascarpone: caramelized pears with Marsala and mascarpone cream 207
  creamy radicchio and mascarpone risotto 63
  tiramisù with raspberries 212
meat and poultry 180–95
melon: cantaloupe melon ice cream 200
  watermelon sorbetto with chocolate chip seeds 203
mint sorbet 200
mozzarella and sun-blushed tomato risotto 56
mozzarella in carrozza 39

mushrooms: chicken and mushroom risotto 68
  mushroom mezzalune 77
  mushroom pizza with basil, chilli and garlic oil 108
  potato and mushroom gratin 156
  quattro stagioni pizza 112–13
  ricotta-stuffed mushrooms 155
  wild mushroom risotto 59
mussels, spaghetti with tomatoes, parsley and 86

O
oil, basil 42
olive oil and garlic bruschetta 31
olives: orange, endive and black olive salad 127
  sautéed peppers with capers and 141
  sweet and sour Sicilian aubergine stew 16
onions: braised lamb cutlets with onions, herbs and olives 185
  fillets of sole in sweet and sour onion marinade 175
  lentils braised with little onions and herbs 163
  rosemary and onion schiacciata 120
  whole onions baked in their skins 131
orange, endive and black olive salad 127

P

pancetta: baked polenta with fontina and pancetta 93

courgettes sautéed with pancetta and thyme 149

see also bacon

pappa al pomodoro 42

Parma ham: mushroom mezzalune 77

with figs and balsamic dressing 23

Parmesan and butter risotto 55

pasta 74–91

cannelloni with ricotta, bitter greens and cherry tomato sauce 78

creamy smoked salmon sauce 85

creamy vodka sauce 89

fresh egg pasta 232

lasagne al forno 90

mushroom mezzalune 77

pasta and bean soup 50

pasta with carbonara sauce 89

pasta with puttanesca sauce 82

roast peppers stuffed with pasta and tomatoes 138

spaghetti with aubergine and tomato sauce 74

spaghetti with mussels, tomatoes and parsley 86

spinach pasta 232

tomato sauce with double basil 80

white spaghetti 81

pastry, shortcrust 211

pears: caramelized pears with Marsala and mascarpone cream 207

peas: Sicilian green vegetables 132

Venetian pea and rice soup 49

peppers: grilled tuna steaks with peperonata 179

red pesto 226

roast peppers stuffed with pasta and tomatoes 138

roasted pepper pizza 107

sautéed peppers with olives and capers 141

pesto: artichoke, pesto and pine nut bruschetta 32

classic pesto 226

red pesto 226

pine nuts: amaretti biscuits with 215

artichoke, pesto and pine nut bruschetta 32

classic pesto 226

red pesto 226

spinach with anchovies and 12

pizza maker's tomato sauce 228

pizzas 102–15

aubergine pizza with bresaola, rocket and Parmesan 111

basic pizza dough 231

Margherita pizza 104

marinara pizza 103

mushroom pizza with basil, chilli and garlic oil 108

potato pizza 115

quattro stagioni pizza 112–13

roasted pepper pizza 107

polenta: baked polenta with fontina and pancetta 93

polenta baked with Italian sausage and cheese 97

soft polenta with sausage ragù 94

pork loin roasted with rosemary and garlic 189

potatoes: the devil's potatoes 159

Italian mixed salad 124

potato and mushroom gratin 156

potato pizza 115

poultry and meat 180–95

prawns, spicy garlic 35

prosciutto and fig bruschetta 36

puttanesca sauce, pasta with 82

Q

quattro stagioni pizza 112–13

R

radicchio: creamy radicchio and mascarpone risotto 63

potato pizza 115

ragù 90, 94

raspberries, tiramisù with 212

la ribollita 45

rice: chicken and mushroom risotto 68

creamy radicchio and mascarpone risotto 63

ham and leek risotto 71

mozzarella and sun-blushed tomato risotto 56

Parmesan and butter risotto 55

red wine risotto 64

seafood and saffron risotto 67

spring risotto with herbs 60

Venetian pea and rice soup 49

wild mushroom risotto 59

ricotta: cannelloni with ricotta, bitter greens and cherry tomato sauce 78

fluffy ricotta fritters 223

pan-fried artichokes with thyme and cool ricotta 135

ricotta-stuffed mushrooms 155

risotto *see* rice

rocket: beefsteak with rocket 190

beetroot, wheat and rocket salad 128

cannelloni with ricotta, bitter greens and cherry tomato sauce 78

grilled fig and prosciutto bruschetta with rocket 36

Roman gnocchi 98

rosemary: *focaccia al rosmarino* 119

rosemary and onion *schiacciata* 120

Sicilian chickpea and rosemary fritters 27

S

saffron: seafood and saffron risotto 67

sage leaves, deep-fried 24

salads 122–9

salsa, caper and mint 176

salt crust, fish baked in 168

sardines baked with garlic, lemon, olive oil and breadcrumbs 171

sauces: béchamel 229

classic pesto 226

creamy smoked salmon 85

creamy vodka 89

pizza maker's tomato 228

red pesto 226

tomato with double basil 80

sausages: grilled sausages with tomato and sage bean stew 194

polenta baked with Italian sausage and cheese 97

soft polenta with sausage ragù 94

schiacciata, rosemary and onion 120

sea bass baked in parchment 172

seafood and saffron risotto 67

semolina, Roman gnocchi with semolina and sage 94

shortcrust pastry 211

Sicilian aubergine stew 16

Sicilian chickpea and rosemary fritters 27

Sicilian green vegetables 132

smoked salmon sauce 85

snacks and antipasti 8–39

sole fillets in sweet and sour onion marinade 175

sorbets: mint sorbet 200

sorbetto al limone 199

watermelon sorbetto with chocolate chip seeds 203

soups 40–51

spaghetti: spaghetti with aubergine and tomato sauce 74

spaghetti with mussels, tomatoes and parsley 86

white spaghetti 81

spinach: spinach broth with egg and cheese 46

spinach pasta 232

spinach with anchovies and pine nuts 12

spring risotto with herbs 60

stews: beef braised in red wine 193

big fish stew 167

grilled sausages with tomato and sage bean stew 194

lentils braised with little onions and herbs 163

sweet and sour Sicilian aubergine stew 16

stock, vegetable 234

sweet and sour Sicilian aubergine stew 16

T

tarts: lemon and almond tart 211

tomato upside-down tart 116

tiramisù with raspberries 212

tomatoes: baked aubergine, tomato, mozzarella and Parmesan 145

big fish stew 167

cannelloni with ricotta, bitter greens and garlic tomato sauce 231

courgettes and tomatoes baked with fontina 147

creamy tomato and bread soup 42

golden aubergines with tomatoes and capers 142

grilled sausages with tomato and sage bean stew 194

grilled tuna steaks with peperonata 179

Margherita pizza 104

marinara pizza 103

mozzarella and sun-blushed tomato risotto 56

mozzarella in carrozza 39

pasta with puttanesca sauce 82

pizza maker's tomato sauce 228

quattro stagioni pizza 112–13

red pesto 226

roast peppers stuffed with pasta and tomatoes 138

roasted pepper pizza 107

slow-roasted tomatoes with garlic and oregano 137

soft polenta with sausage ragù 94

spaghetti with aubergine and tomato sauce 74

spaghetti with mussels, tomatoes and parsley 86

spicy garlic prawns with tomatoes and chickpeas 35

sweet and sour Sicilian aubergine stew 16

tomato sauce with double basil 80

tomato upside-down tart 116

traditional peasant tomato and garlic bruschetta 28

tuna: grilled tuna steaks with peperonata 179

oven-baked tuna with salsa 176

V

vegetables: la ribollita 45

spring risotto with herbs 60

vegetable stock 234

see also individual vegetables

Venetian pea and rice soup 49

vodka sauce, creamy 89

W

watermelon sorbetto with chocolate chip seeds 203

wheat, beetroot and rocket salad 128

white spaghetti 81

wine: beef braised in red wine 193

caramelized pears with Marsala and mascarpone cream 207

carrots with olive oil and Marsala 152

mint sorbet 200

red wine risotto 64

zabaglione 204

Z

zabaglione 204

credits

All the recipes featured in this book are by Maxine Clark except the following, which are by Silvana Franco:

Aubergine with Bresaola, Rocket and Parmesan
Basic Pizza Dough
Creamy Smoked Salmon Sauce
Creamy Vodka Sauce
Marinara Pizza
Mushroom Mezzalune
Mushroom Pizza with Basil, Chilli and Garlic Oil
Pasta with Carbonara Sauce
Pasta with Puttanesca Sauce
Quattro Stagioni Pizza
Roasted Pepper Pizza
Tomato Sauce with Double Basil
White Spaghetti

Photographs

Martin Brigdale
Pages 2, 10, 17, 21, 22, 43, 44, 47, 48, 51, 53 centre, 53 right, 54, 57, 58, 61, 62, 65, 66, 69, 70, 72, 75, 87, 91, 92, 95, 99, 101 centre, 101 right, 105, 114, 117, 118, 125, 126, 144, 164, 165 left, 165 right, 173, 174, 178, 181 centre, 181 right, 184, 191, 195, 197 left, 198, 205, 210, 213, 222, 227, 233, 235, 237

Peter Cassidy
Front endpaper left, 13, 14, 18, 24, 40, 41 centre, 41 right, 53 left, 73 left, 73 right, 79, 96, 100, 101 left, 121, 123 all,129, 130, 133, 134, 136–137, 139, 140, 143, 146–147, 148, 151, 153, 154, 157, 158, 161, 162, 165 centre, 166, 169, 170, 177, 182–183, 187, 188, 192, 196, 206–207, 209, 217, 225 all, 238

William Lingwood
Pages 9 centre, 73 centre, 76, 80, 81, 83, 84–85, 86, 88–89, 102–103, 106, 109, 110–111, 112–113, 138, 145, 180, 211, 228–229, 230–231, 232

Gus Filgate
Pages 8, 9 left, 25, 26, 29, 30, 33, 34, 37, 38, 122

Jean Cazals
Pages 201, 202, 203, 214, 218, 221

James Merrell
Pages 11, 135, 181 left, 224

Chris Tubbs
Front endpaper right, pages 3, 7

Alan Williams
Pages 6, 199, 240

Francesca Yorke
Pages 9 right, 197 centre, 197 right

Nicky Dowey
Pages 30, 64

David Munns
Pages 52, 107

Pia Tryde
Back endpaper right, page 4

Caroline Arber
Page 98

Christopher Drake
Back endpaper left

David Loftus
Page 5

Debi Treloar
Page 1

Ian Wallace
Page 41 left